BE NOT AFRAID

"These things I have spoken unto you, that in me ye might have peace. In the world ye shall have tribulation: but be of good cheer; I have overcome the world" . . . Jesus Christ
[John 16:33]

By Alfred Udobong
Global Manifestation Ministries

Pastor Alfred Udobong,
P.O.Box 1974
Silver Spring, MD 20915
gmm_ministries@yahoo.com

Global Manifestation Ministries.
ISBN 0-9772789-0-5

Cover Photo: Ken Malone
Designed and Produced by Truth Communications
www.publishingtruth.com

Printed in the United States of America

Be Not Afraid

You shall not be afraid of the terror by night, nor of the arrow that flies by day, nor of the pestilence that walks in darkness, nor of the destruction that lays waste at noonday. A thousand may fall at your side. And ten thousand at your right hand; but it shall not come near you. Only with your eyes shall you look and see the reward of the wicked˜ (Psalm 91:5-8 NKJV).

Do not be afraid of sudden terror, nor of trouble from the wicked when it comes. For the Lord will be your confidence, and will keep your foot from being caught˜ (Proverbs 3:25-26 NKJV).

The apostle Paul told Timothy that God, Hath not given us [believers] the spirit of fear; but of power, and of love, and of a sound mind˜ (2 Timothy 1:7).

Do not be afraid of their threats nor be troubled˜ (1 Peter 3:14 NKJV).

God is ready today to fulfill in you what He plans for your life. You can hold on to Him today. You can be very victorious despite all odds. All you need is self-discovery and God's positioning.

Dedication

I dedicate this book with thanks giving to the Holy Spirit, for His prompting and all that I know and that which I will come to know that He has done for me.

I also dedicate this to my dear wife Edna –thank you for the love and for unselfishly allowing me to give myself to His services.

I want to also give my special thanks to all others I cannot mention for their contributions to making the commission of God upon my life a success.

Be Not Afraid

By Alfred Udobong
Global Manifestation Ministries

Table of Contents

Introduction 5

Acknowledgment 11

Chapter 1: Be Armed 13

Chapter 2: Stirring the Nest 25

Chapter 3: In Nothing Be Terrified 37

Chapter 4: Heroes of Faith: A Study of Hebrews 11 . . . 49

Chapter 5: Our Defense 57

Chapter 6: Scriptural Assurance To Encourage Us 81

Chapter 7: Something Must Give Way 93

Chapter 8: Thirty-six Tactics Used by the Devil 103

Chapter 9: The Road To Calvary's Cross 113

Chapter 10: The Place of Prayer 119

Conclusion 137

About the Author 141

Introduction

4

Introduction

Fear is a stopper of all good intentions. It is a restrainer of good minds and deeds—a blinder to glory, peace, blessings, success, and the authority of Christians. It is one of the devices the Devil uses to cause havoc in the world and in the lives of believers. Almost every generation has come to a crossroad of faith as a result of fear. The disciples of Christ Jesus experienced this silent killer of the Devil in their lives and ministry, as did others in the Bible.

Let us look at some words from the Bible about how, to deal with fear. "I tell you, my friends, do not be afraid of those who kill the body and after that can do no more. But I will show you whom you should fear: fear him who, after the killing of the body, has power to throw you into hell. Yes, I tell you, fear him (Luke 12:4-5 NIV).

Jesus Christ made this statement to His disciples and to the others who followed Him to hear His teachings. Yet, this statement is also for us today if we are to have any meaningful progress in all that we do. Fear should no longer keep us back.

Trouble is a nest shaker. It tests our spiritual foundation and investigates our potential and standard of faith. We all should realize that we cannot stop trouble from happening to us, but we can definitely refuse to be overtaken by it. This is done through determination, dedication, and absolutely relying on Jesus Christ—on all of His words for help and victory.

Look at what God told the prophets of old about fear,

I, even I, am he who comforts you. Who are you that you fear mortal men, the son of men, who are but grass, that you forget the Lord your Maker, who stretched out the heavens and laid the foundations of the earth, that you live in constant terror every day because of the wrath of the oppressor, who is bent on destruction? For where is the wrath of the oppressor? The cowering prisoners will soon be set free; they will not die in their dungeon, nor will they lack bread. For I am the Lord your God, who churns up the sea so that its waves roar—the Lord Almighty is his name. I have put my words in your mouth and covered you with the shadow of my hand—I who set the heavens in place, who laid the foundations of the earth, and who say Zion, "You are my people" (Isaiah 51:12-16 NIV).

To Jeremiah He said, "Be not afraid of their faces: for I am with thee to deliver thee" (Jeremiah 1:8).

To Ezekiel He said,

You, son of man, do not be afraid of them or their words. Do not be afraid, though briers and thorns are all around you and you live among scorpions. Do not be afraid of what they say or terrified by them, though they are a rebellious house. You must speak my words to them, whether they listen or fail to listen, for they are rebellious. But you, son of man, listen to what I say to you. Do not rebel like that rebellious house, open your mouth and eat what I give you (Ezekiel 2:6-8 NIV).

This same word is given to you today. Jesus said, "Man shall not live by bread alone, but by every word that proceedeth out of the mouth of God" (Matthew 4:4). The greatest weapon against fear throughout the ages has been

God's word of assurance to all people. In our time, this is expressed through the manifestation of love in Christ Jesus.

The greatest support that any person can rely upon on this planet earth is the love that God has for mankind. Only the love of the almighty God—as expressed through our Lord and Savior Jesus Christ—has the power to change all things. His love has changed our world before, and His love is sustaining the world today. This love has hope, power, assurance, assistance, and life embedded in it for all that will ever receive it. This love is pregnant with all the blessings that the world will ever need. Our world will be completely changed if we all will accept the challenges of the love that God has freely given us.

For God so love the world, that he gave his only begotten Son, that whosoever believeth in him should not perish, but have everlasting life. For God sent not his Son into the world to condemn the world; but that the world through him might be saved. He that believeth on him is not condemned: but he that believeth not is condemned already, because he hath not believed in the name of the only begotten Son of God (John 3:16-18).

The love of God shuts all doors against all forms of satanic and human condemnation, and it enhances our values in all things. Love is the identity of God that He uses to reach the world.

Love requires complete surrender to the almighty in order to be most effective. Remember Christ Jesus surrendered Himself for the world.

Jonathan surrendered his claim to the throne of his father to David. David accepted the love that Jonathan offered, and inherited the kingdom after the demise of King

Saul. The same will be true for everyone that accepts the love of God through Christ Jesus. We will inherit all of His promises here on earth and afterward in heaven.

This is the value of love: you inherit a promise. Love gives you all things—including open access to heavenly blessings in Christ Jesus. As 1 Corinthians 13:4-7 teaches, "Love is patient, love is kind. It does not envy, it does not boast, it is not proud. It is not rude, it is not self-seeking, it is not easily angered, it keeps no record of wrongs. Love does not delight in evil but rejoices with the truth. It always protects, always trusts, always hopes, and always perseveres."

Through love, God asks us not to be afraid of the things we see or experience daily, and urges us to go forward in faith and assurance of His presence and protection.

All the promises of God to mankind are embedded in His unconditional love to the entire world. But to be a full beneficiary of this love, there are some things we have to do. First, we must realize that the Devil is primarily out to stop believers from obtaining the fullness of God's love through fear. Fear is the greatest hindrance to faith, and it is the agent that Satan uses to compose all the falsehoods that lead Christians astray. To work in faith is to put fear in check—only then can we benefit fully in the great love of God.

Second, we must understand that through fear, many are subjected to untold afflictions. In fact, we often become slaves to the effects of these afflictions, which delays our healing, peace, and deliverance. Fear stops us from yielding fruit, hinders and kills our love and progress, torments us, holds us in captivity, hinders the Word of God in our lives, and stops us from being fulfilled as Christians.

Wordsworth once wrote, "Fear has a hundred eyes and all agree." Whenever we are hindered by fear, we are robbed of our testimonies in Christ Jesus. The children of Israel moved with joy toward the Promised Land after obtaining a word from God. However, on their way, they got stuck by the Red Sea. Bound with fear, they stopped. But after consultation and prayers, God instructed them to move on, and the word of victory soon came.

Moses said unto the people, Fear ye not, stand still, and see the salvation of the Lord, which he will shew to you to day: for the Egyptians whom ye have seen to day, ye shall see them again no more for ever. The Lord shall fight for you, and ye shall hold your peace. And the Lord said unto Moses, Wherefore criest thou unto me? speak unto the children of Israel, that they go forward (Exodus 14:13-15).

God's promises for you are true, and you can receive them all. Whether your troubles are spiritual or physical, you can have triumph over all of them by His grace.

So enjoy reading this book, and allow these powerful words from the throne of grace to encourage you greatly.

- "Ye shall not need to fight in this battle: set yourselves, stand ye still, and see the salvation of the Lord with you, O Judah and Jerusalem: fear not, nor be dismayed; to morrow go out against them, for the Lord will be with you" (2 Chronicles 20:17).

- "He answered, Fear not: for they that be with us are more than they that be with them" (2 Kings 6:16).

- "The very hairs of your head are all numbered. Fear ye not therefore, ye are of more value than many sparrows" (Matthew 10:30-31).

• "These things I have spoken unto you, that in me ye might have peace. In the world ye shall have tribulation: but be of good cheer; I have overcome the world" (John 16:33).

God is waiting for you to step out in faith in order to give you the victory promised, just as He did for the Israelites on their way to the Promised Land. By reading this book, you are launching yourself into the victorious battle for your destiny. People of God, despite what you're passing through right now, Christ Jesus has settled the results in your favor.

Amen. Peace.

ACKNOWLEDGMENT

We all search earnestly for answers to our various life challenging questions. What a refreshment it will bring to our soul when we surprisingly discover that we have already gotten the answers in our hands. "When the Lord turned again the captivity of Zion, we were like them that dream, then was our mouth filled with laughter, and our tongue with singing, then said them among the heathen, the Lord hath done great things for them, the Lord had done great things for us, were we are glad " Psalms 147:1-3

His beauty will replace your ashes and you will be raised from your present zero level to being a hero. Amazingly what started as a personal testimony in the school of faith with Pastor Alfred Udobong is now turned into an inspiring writing, and will now bless whosoever reads this book. The Book BE NOT AFRAID is written through the power of the Holy Spirit, that it will help you to understand and apply the hidden wisdom of God.

Knowing that the days are evil, Pastor Alfred has taken deep breath from the Holy Spirit to put down this thoughts for any one who will want to hear what the Holy Spirit is doing and revealing to those who will let Him lead them. This is your moment, TAKE IT BY FORCE. The writer was not telling you story but rather he shared in this book his challenging and personal miracles that support his claim and experience he had with God.

This book shows you the way to know the Lord; he went deep to teach you about spiritual warfare, and the material that turns your faith loose to move your mountain out of your way. He wrote in detail about holiness without which no one will see God. If really you are interested in making heaven at last, you must read this book so that you will have the theological understanding about God's love and judgment.

This book will take you higher into the realm of a higher spiritual authority today. Behold I have given you the keys of the kingdom of God, whatsoever you bind on earth is bound in heaven and whatsoever you loose on earth is loosed in heaven. Because this book compacts various topics and ideas that will make God's power available to you. I therefore recommend this precious book to ministers and Christians who are in dare need of help from above. I pray also that as Pastor Alfred yields his life that the Holy Spirit will anoint his mind and hands for greater revelation in the word of God. and may all readers of this book receive more than they have expected. May the Lord receive all the glory.

Bishop (Dr.) Emmanuel C. Okoli
President,
Fresh Anointing World Outreach Ministries Intl.
Atlanta Georgia.

Chapter 1
Be Armed

Surely temptations will come, trials will come, and you will meet pitfalls on your way to heaven—but don't give up the fight. Christ Jesus was tempted in every way, but never gave up the fight for our redemption. He persevered until victory was won on the cross. That victory was for us—for you—then, today, and forever. Stand on that victory. Activate it in your life and remind the Devil about it. Face your problems with that triumph in mind, and resolve to stand in faith against all the foes that rise up against you.

There is nothing impossible for the person that believes in the saving grace of Christ Jesus. Miracles are as real today as they were in years gone by. Yet, miracles are directly proportional to the level of your belief. Your trust in God is paramount to receiving anything from God.

We must believe in the God of miracles, and expect to experience at least one miracle every day. This may sound excessive, but Christians should understand that we take many of the things that constitute a miracle for granted.

For example, salvation is a miracle. Life—in itself—is a miracle. Deliverance, healing, good health, and contentment are miracles—as are having a good job, having all of our needs met, and having the ability to live a godly life. All are God's miraculous and abundant provision for His children.

Beginning today, increase your belief in miracles—especially as you read this book. It could turn things around for you forever. The strength of your faith is very important to you and to others around you—it will either encourage or dishearten other Christians.

The pages of the Bible are filled with proof of God's miraculous power, and the Devil is frightened when you believe in Him. Remember the Devil also believes and trembles. James 2:19 (NIV) states, "You believe that there is one God. Good! Even the demons believe that—and shudder." Your believing had to be distinguished with a daily trust and total submission to Christ Jesus. This is because, as Proverbs 24:16 teaches, "Though a righteous man falls seven times, he rises again." The person who truly believes in Jesus Christ is impossible for the Enemy to defeat, even though he falls several times. You have to defeat all fears of falling and rising and look ahead for the saving grace from heaven.

Therefore, don't be terrified by the things you see, but rejoice about what you are becoming through Christ Jesus. Whatever you see today is temporal—it will surely pass away. Remember that after each fall—Christ lifts you up. And after each victory comes a celebration. Your present position or problem is not your last point in life—there is a place God is planning for you that you will soon discover and move into.

The Devil is like a roaring lion, looking for whom he will devour (1 Peter 5:8). The righteous are tempted every day, in every way. That is why we must live by faith in Christ Jesus at all times. And we should always give thanks to Him, because He will not forsake us in times of need or trouble; neither will He forget us when we have gained the victory. He stands with His people forever.

Your attitude concerning any problem will be based on

your level of knowledge and understanding of the Enemy's tactics. Problems cannot be solved on the same level of awareness as which they were created—you must attain a higher level of knowledge to solve them. That level is found within the spiritual realm, which is the parent of all physical things. And prayer is the spiritual battle that shapes physical realities.

Therefore, the determination to conquer your problem is the first condition necessary for your victory—you must want to overcome it, even if it means challenging and increasing your knowledge, and taking your battle to the spiritual level. And you should realize that the Devil would not fold his hands and watch you succeed. He does not care about God's promises for you, but works to impede their fulfillment in your life (Genesis 3:1-5).

To break Satan's influence, delay tactics, and outright destructive activity toward God's plans, there are some very important things you have to know and do.

1. Be born again.

Speaking to a religious leader called Nicodemus, Jesus said, "Except a man is born again, he cannot see the kingdom of God. . . . Except a man is born of water and of the Spirit, he cannot enter into the kingdom of God. . . . Marvel not that I say unto you, ye must be born again" (John 3:3,5,7). Being born again is a must. It is a heavenly command.

Being *born again* involves accepting Christ Jesus as your only Lord and Savior, and deliberately deciding to reject your former way of living in order to put the biblical pattern for conducting your life into practice. This involves a shift in focus—seeking to please only Christ Jesus in all things, and considering all things from the standpoint of Scripture. You become exclusively accountable to God, and are focused on making heaven the goal and reward of this present life.

Being born again means seeking to live a profitable life that will please God. However, that only occurs when we recognize that this life is temporal, and that there is another life awaiting us—whether that is a better, more meaningful eternity with Christ Jesus in heaven, or a bitter existence for the lost in hell. God Almighty, the Creator of all things, will ask each of us to give an account of how we conducted ourselves and how we made use of the numerous opportunities He gave us. He expects us to look to Him for guidance and direction daily, and to obey His commands. That is the whole essence of being born again—God's love and assistance in all things.

If you want to be victorious in this life, accept Christ Jesus as your only Lord and Savior, and you will be on your way to the greatest victory you have ever experienced. You can only become a child of God by being born again—it cannot be achieved by church attendance, observing religious rites, or having religious friends or parents

2. Repent of all known sin.

Christ Jesus is calling the whole world, big and small, religious or not, to repent. The whole creation will be ruined if we don't repent. We are what we are today by His righteousness.

Christ Jesus said, "Except ye repent, ye shall likewise perish" (Luke 13:3).

On another occasion, Peter said, "Repent, and be baptized every one of you in the name of Jesus Christ for the remission of sins, and ye shall receive the gift of the Holy Ghost" (Acts 2:38). Genuine repentance should be followed by water baptism through immersion.

And in 1 John 1:8-9 we are taught, "If we say that we have no sin, we deceive ourselves, and the truth is not in us. If we confess our sins, he is faithful and just to forgive us our sins, and to cleanse us from all unrighteousness."

A successful life with Christ Jesus requires daily self-examination. A successful Christian is one that questions his or her heart every day, and tries—through prayer and the leading of the Holy Spirit—to make all of his or her thoughts and ways to conform to the will of Christ Jesus. Repentance comes in whenever we find ourselves falling away from the biblical standard.

Repentance means seeking mercy from God and turning away from the gates of destruction. A sinner is a ready, captive tool in the hands of the Devil. Therefore, a Christian must repent of his or her sins in order to not grow blind and be accustomed to sin. It does not matter how many years he or she has been a Christian, or what he or she has done in the past. There are simply too many things that can hurt our faith and make us sin—we cannot ignore our weaknesses.

It is this self-examination that reveals were we have strayed from the ways of the living God, and prayer helps us to return to His love, because in prayers, He reveals our shortcomings. Today is the best day to correct our mistakes through genuine repentance. We must decide to keep away from such things from now on. As long as you are alive, you can repent. However, tomorrow might be too late for you—for you are not guaranteed another day.

Therefore, since you may not have this opportunity tomorrow, take advantage of the opportunity right now and repent. Ask God to help you correct the wrongs you've committed against Him, yourself and others. "For all have sinned and fall short of the glory of God" (Romans 3:23 NIV).

 And "the wages of sin is dead, but the gift of God is eternal life in Christ Jesus" (Romans 6:23 NIV).

3. Acquire knowledge.

Knowledge is power and the catalyst of all changes. Acquiring knowledge requires you to invest in the experiences that will expose you to it, and being disciplined in following the principles you learn. The things you know will distinguish you from others. The more you know, the better your ability to succeed.

Spiritual battles are fought with spiritual weapons—and require spiritual knowledge. The greatest spiritual weapon a person can ever possess is the Spirit of the living God. The Spirit of God helps us in our infirmities and reveals all things to us. He also guards us as we fight our battles and live our lives.

In 2 Timothy 2:15, Paul instructed Timothy, "Study to shew thyself approved unto God, a workman that needeth not to be ashamed, rightly dividing the word of truth." You acquire knowledge through a systematic study of the Bible, through reading of Christian literature and listening to biblical teaching, and through your everyday association with other Christians. Confidence, boldness, determination, wealth, and good health are all products of that knowledge.

However, without Christ Jesus, you can do very little with all the knowledge you have. The Holy Spirit must transform your intellectual knowledge into spiritual reality. Only He can enhance your knowledge and reward you adequately. Without Him, you cannot achieve success—which means frustration and eventual destruction.

4. Know the Enemy fighting you.

Knowledge of the Enemy and his strategies will help you prepare for battle. Remember, before God gave the Israelites the Promised Land, He accepted Moses to send an advance team to the land to spy it out. They went to evaluate the capability and strength of the enemy.

Consider carefully the things they were ask to check out in the land. If we want to overrun the Enemy, then we must study who he is and what weapons he employs. Numbers 13:17-20 describes the mandate,

> Moses sent them to spy out the land of Canaan, and said unto them, Get you up this way southward, and go up into the mountain: And see the land, what it is, and the people that dwelleth therein, whether they be strong or weak, few or many; And what the land is that they dwell in, whether it be good or bad; and what cities they be that they dwell in, whether in tents, or in strong holds; And what the land is, whether it be fat or lean, whether there be wood therein, or not. And be ye of good courage, and bring of the fruit of the land.

In Luke 14:31, Christ Jesus spoke about seeking out advance knowledge of the enemy's weapons, "What king, going to make war against another king, sitteth not down first, and consulteth whether he be able with ten thousand to meet him that cometh against him with twenty thousand?"

We must understand that we are fighting a very old, experienced, and strategic enemy called Satan or the Devil. But our God—who is above all things, created all things, and knows all things—has all the information about him, his tactics, and weaponry. And He has made them available to all His children through Christ Jesus.

5. Know the weapons that the Enemy can't resist—and use them.

All wars involve weapons and leave behind victims. God—not willing that we be victims in these spiritual battles—makes an enormous cache of weapons available to us so that we may face any battle at any time. His saving blood, name, and all the contents of the Bible (the Word of God) comprise our impressive arsenal. Your ability to use them properly will prove your victory.

These weapons are for us to use, but it is very important that we know how to use them. Mastery of them depends on you—how you train yourself and how often you use them. These weapons are spiritual, irresistible, and are very effective. Our Enemy is spiritual and needs to be fought spiritually, and all Christians are called to rise and fight him. Christ Jesus made a public shame of the Enemy on the cross of Calvary, and He is calling on us today to arm ourselves with that testimony and to do the same in His name. Colossians 2:16 (NIV) says, "Having disarmed the powers and authorities, he made a public spectacle of them, triumphing over them by the cross."

In 2 Corinthians 10:3-6, Paul writes,

Though we walk in the flesh, we do not war after the flesh: (for the weapons of our warfare are not carnal, but mighty through God to the pulling down of strong holds;) casting down imaginations, and every high thing that exalteth itself against the knowledge of God, and bringing into captivity every thought to the obedience of Christ; and having in a readiness to revenge all disobedience, when your obedience is fulfilled.

And in Ephesians 6:10-11, he writes also,

Finally, my brethren, be strong in the Lord, and in the power of his might. Put on the whole Armour of God, that ye may be able to stand against the wiles of the devil.

Never go to war without being armed. David despised the physical weapons of Saul when facing Goliath, because he knew he was spiritually armed and prepared through his personal testimony and the knowledge of the God of Israel. He said, "You come against me with sword and spear and javelin, but I come against you in the name of the Lord Almighty, the God of the armies of Israel, whom you have defied" (1 Samuel 17:45 NIV).

6. Know how to pray

Christ Jesus places much importance on prayer, and committed a great part of His ministry to prayers in divers places. Speaking in Matthew 6:5-7, Jesus mentioned prayers seven times.

Prayer changes all things—it frustrates the plans of the Devil, and quickens the plans of God in all things. Prayer has no boundaries, and God answers all prayers according to His will. There are various types of prayers—petition, supplication, thanksgiving, warfare, intercession, resistance, acceptance, etc. In Philippians 4:6, we are advised to pray all manners of prayers, so some examples of different prayers have been listed later in this book to assist you.

Christ Jesus prayed all these types of prayers during His time on earth, and also taught His disciples to do the same, and He had tremendous results. The apostles followed in His footsteps and also had great success. Luke 11:1 (NIV) has this report, "One day Jesus was praying in a certain place. When he finished, one of his disciples said to him, 'Lord, teach us to pray, just as John taught his disciples.'"

We are encouraged to do the same, and there is no doubt we will have the same result when we pray. As James 5:16 admonishes, "The effectual fervent prayer of a righteous man availeth much."

Let us examine what the men who set themselves against Jeremiah wanted, and what prayers the prophet made when he was in trouble. These enemies watched and waited for him to slip—wanting to prevail against him and exact revenge. Yet, Jeremiah 20:10-11 records his prayers against his adversaries,

I heard the defaming of many, fear on every side. Report, say they, and we will report it. All my familiars watched for my halting, saying, Peradventure he will be enticed, and we shall prevail against him, and we shall take our revenge on him. But the Lord is with me as a mighty terrible one: therefore my persecutors shall stumble, and they shall not prevail: they shall be greatly ashamed; for they shall not prosper: their everlasting confusion shall never be forgotten.

7. Know the power of the God you serve.

The greatest thing Christ Jesus came to do on earth was to set us free from all forms of evil, darkness, and satanic afflictions; and to show us the way back to our Maker. This was achieved through the shedding of His blood on the cross of Calvary. Through this, we became one of the Father's beloved children. He taught, "The thief cometh not, but for to steal, and to kill, and to destroy: I am come that [you] might have life, and that [you] might have it more abundantly" (John 10:10).

Also, we know that, "The Lord is not slack concerning his promise, as some men count slackness; but is longsuffering to us-ward, not willing that any should perish, but that all should come to repentance" (2 Peter 3:9)

Let us look at some critical words from the Bible about His power. Romans 14:11 teaches, "As I live, saith the Lord, every knee shall bow to me, and every tongue shall confess to God." And in Philippians 2:10-11 (NIV), "That at the name of Jesus every knee should bow, of things in heaven, and things in earth, and things under the earth. And that every tongue should confess that Jesus Christ is Lord, to the glory of God the Father."

John, speaking in Revelation 5:11-13 about the power of Christ Jesus, said,

> **I beheld, and I heard the voice of many angels round about the throne and the beasts and the elders: and the number of them was ten thousand times ten thousand, and thousands of thousands; saying with a loud voice, Worthy is the Lamb that was slain to receive power, and riches, and wisdom, and strength, and honour, and glory, and blessing. And every creature which is in heaven, and on the earth, and under the earth, and such as are in the sea, and all that are in them, heard I saying, Blessing, and honour, and glory, and power, be unto him that sitteth upon the throne, and unto the Lamb for ever and ever.**

Every promise from God is real, true, and available to everyone that will believe and accept His ways. He is willing to do much more than you could ever imagine—especially as you trust Him in all things. The power of our God is not limited to this sphere alone—heaven and earth, men and angels, anything on earth and those under earth, must respect and bow to His name.

The power of our God is not limited to these sphere alone, heaven and earth, men and angels, any thing on earth and those under earth, must respects and bows to that name.

Chapter 2
Stirring the Nest

We know from Deuteronomy 32:10-14 that promotion can also come through trials and temptations.

He found him in a desert land, and in the waste howling wilderness; he led him about, he instructed him, he kept him as the apple of his eye. As an eagle stirreth up her nest, fluttereth over her young, spreadeth abroad her wings, taketh them, beareth them on her wings: so the Lord alone did lead him, and there was no strange god with him. He made him ride on the high places of the earth, that he might eat the increase of the fields; and he made him to suck honey out of the rock, and oil out of the flinty rock; butter of kine, and milk of sheep, with fat of lambs, and rams of the breed of Bashan, and goats, with the fat of kidneys of wheat; and thou didst drink the pure blood of the grape.

As Act 14:21-22 (NKJV) explains, "They returned . . . strengthening the souls of the disciples, exhorting them to continue in the faith, and saying, 'We must through many tribulations enter the kingdom of God.'"

Certainly, trials and temptations are not desirable in any way. However, behind every trial or temptation that a born again child of God undergoes, there is a great treasure of reward from our Father.

No one ever prays for a problem; rather, we pray for

 blessings and deliverance. Yet, sometimes we face a problem that varies greatly from our prayers. What we must understand is that God's goodwill is with us, whether we are conscious of it or not; and that our spiritual promotion—or maturity—comes consciously through facing our problems with faith in Him.

When there is a need to be filled for His plans to be carried out, God raises up someone to perform it. This has been God's method throughout all generations. God does not promote anyone simply because they ask or cry out for prominence in His kingdom's work. Rather, God uses the unspecified avenues of hardship, challenge, and suffering in order to prepare a person to fulfill a particular purpose.

Before promotion comes, there must be some form of training and examination. God will always prepare the Christians He intends to use. Each training session varies depending on the work to be performed, and might come in the form of sickness or sorrow—whether that be personal hardship or that of loved ones. Their purpose is not to bring you down from the lofty heights that God has placed you. Rather, they will bring you up to the higher place of God for your life—if you will pass the test, learn the inherent lessons, imitate His ways, renounce your doubts, and be willing to follow the Master's steps.

Out of love, God told Lot that He wanted to destroy the sinful city of Sodom, and that Lot should flee to a nearby mountain. But Lot preferred a plain, which was closer and less stressful a journey. The ways of men are surely ways of destruction. But before he could reach his proposed destination, his wife had become a pillar of salt. Thereafter he decided to follow the instructions of God. He finally made it to the mountains, realizing late the benefits of obeying God, by the bitter lesson of loosing his lifelong companion and helpmate.

Please note that not all suffering is training for God's promotion, the Devil also tempts us in his own ways. The trials and temptations you are facing as a Christian—such as delays, obstacles, sickness, and lack—can also be the result of satanic manipulations. Remember Job's suffering was not intended by God, but it happened because the Enemy had God's approval. The Devil had to obtain a pass from God before he could reach on to Job.

When you allow the trials to overwhelm you and lose your focus on God's greater purpose, you will surely fail and lose the inherent glory. You need to develop an overcoming spirit when faced with any kind of difficulty in life—just as Job did when he said, "Though he slay me, yet will I trust in him" (Job 13:15). He referred to God, even though God was not the one slaying him. This is the spirit that Job possessed throughout his trails—and he prevailed. He refused to give up to the calamities that befell him, irrespective of their source.

Know that right inside that problem you are facing is God's hidden place for your escape and your subsequent promotion in life. God always provides a hidden place, plans for your success, a course for spiritual breakthrough, and a solid foundation for your future. Always remember to ask God to open your eyes so that you may see beyond whatever problem you are facing, and so that He can help you to overcome it. Decide not to fight with blind eyes. Ask God to open your eyes to see the real enemy behind the mask. It might be someone you never thought. This will enable you to face the battle with greater determination.

In a battlefield, Joshua had an unusual encounter and had to probe further.

When Joshua was near Jericho, he looked up and saw a man standing in front of him with a drawn sword in his hand. Joshua went up to him and asked, "Are you for us or for our enemies?" "Neither," he replied, "but as commander of the army of the Lord I have now come." Then Joshua fell facedown to the ground in reverence, and asked him, "What message does my Lord have for his servant?" (Joshua 5:13-14 NIV).

Job saw spiritual prosperity in everything that came to him, and he decided to honor the Lord despite all of the advice from his friends and dear wife. And God made a way for him to be seven times more blessed in all things than he was before.

Noah also obeyed the instructions of the Lord despite the mockery of other people, and saw exceeding greatness because of it.

Moses saw that through identifying with God's people—though sorrow and suffering accompanied him—he became what God wanted him to be. By defending the Hebrew slave and killing the Egyptian guard, he chose to leave his opulent position in the palace and to become an ordinary man. And God made him a man of substance and of great respect.

David—through the trials of his life and his fights in the forest with bears and lions—became qualified to face Goliath in a battle to liberate Israel. He defeated the champion of the Philistines and became both the popular leader of the people and their God-given king.

There is always a choice to make in all things. Why not make a decision to face your problems and overcome them in a manner that will gain you the inherent promotion and blessings He desires for you? As Samson said in Judges

14:14, "Out of the eater came forth meat, and out of the strong came forth sweetness." Kill the lion—face your trials in a godly manner—and you will find honey in its carcass.

Whom the Lord loveth he chasteneth, and scourgeth every son whom he receiveth. If ye endure chastening, God dealeth with you as with sons; for what son is he whom the father chasteneth not? But if ye be without chastisement, whereof all are partakers, then are ye bastards, and not sons. Furthermore we have had fathers of our flesh which corrected us, and we gave them reverence: shall we not much rather be in subjection unto the Father of spirits, and live? (Hebrews 12:6-9).

As a Christian, trials, temptations, and problems will develop the following in you:

1. A strong faith in God and in His ability.

We know from Hebrews 11:6, "Without faith it is impossible to please him." God respects men of faith, while the Devil is greatly afraid of them. That is because you can only truly impact your world through faith in the Lord Jesus Christ.

We as Christians will never know our full potential unless we apply faith to our daily endeavors. Faith is not a risk, but a strong trust and a continuous hope in the saving grace of our Lord Jesus Christ. And it is developed primarily through some kind of difficulty. Paul said faith without work is dead when it abides alone.

A faithless Christian cannot progress in any way, and is generally very defeated. However, great faith can move mountains, level valleys, clear all the obstacles from our path daily, and bring miracles. Faith can buoy a load of problems as a ship floats on the ocean. The faithful Christian always has great testimonies about God's goodness, because faith is peace with God.

People of faith are not pushovers in any area of life. When we stand up to declare Christ Jesus in the face of opposition, we are activating our faith. And remember, faith can only work when activated.

"We are always confident, knowing that, whilst we are at home in the body, we are absent from the Lord: for we walk by faith, not by sight" (2 Corinthians 5:6-7).

2. A strong confidence and trust in the absolute power and ability of God to make you successful in all things of life.

If through trials and temptations we develop this faith in God, nothing else can shake our foundation in life. By this we know that God is with us, and we can say confidently, "If God be for us, who can be against us?" (Romans 8:31).

Paul originally made that statement after passing through many trials. When you experience God's victory after your first encounter with suffering, you will learn that subsequent trials will also lead to high praise and thanksgiving to the living God though you don't pray for any trouble. Knowing that it is just a matter of time and God will deliver you from the evil circumstances will help you sail through the trial to the glorious land. We can glory in tribulation, knowing that it will give birth to patience, experience, hope in God, and boundless joy (Romans 5:1-5).

Nahum 1:7 teaches, "The Lord is good, a strong hold in the day of trouble; and he knoweth them that trust in him." Trusting God is the bedrock of a daily life of miracles.

Practice it and you will see them flow in from every direction. Though time solves all problems, there are also instances of immediate response from God. Hold on to your confidence in His ability, whether your case requires time or an immediate response. Your miracle is on the way.

3. Knowledge of the methodology of Christ Jesus and what it requires to be a perfect child of the living God.

Knowledge rightly acquired is indispensable because it is power, it can change all things about you. There are three basic methods of learning:

A. *Learning by observation.* Observe godly people close to you and ask them questions about what they are going through and what they have gone through previously in life. This is called mentorship. You also have many stories in the Bible to learn from.

B. *Learning from books.* Read about people's experiences in good and in difficult situations in life.

C. *Learning through personal experience.* God uses the last method only when you refuse to learn from the previous two methods. Observation and reading are the best and simplest ways of learning. Yet, God will use the last option in order to get you on the path of acceptance and obedience to His commands.

Ask yourself this question, "What knowledge does God want me to have in this problem?"

The Bible encourages us to grow in knowledge as we grow in grace (1 Peter 1:13; 2 Peter 3:18). This is because knowledge comes from the Holy Spirit, and a person of knowledge will possess strength and great courage (Proverbs 24:5). Remember, wise men make knowledge their stronghold, and the foolish play away their time and fail to acquire it. Lack of knowledge always leads to destruction (Hosea 4:6).

Knowledge will lift you up and bring you promotion, perfect confidence, and a strong faith in God. Application of knowledge is the weapon of the wise, and it is what makes the difference between a foolish failure and a wise success.

4. The increase in knowledge with a correspon-ding growth in wisdom will get you to the pinnacle of life faster.

The wisdom referred to here is godly wisdom. Without wisdom, you will make decisions that are detrimental to your faith—despite all the knowledge you have. Wisdom is the principal thing.

Through His wisdom, God sustains and continuously replenishes all things He created from the beginning of creation. God made Solomon the king of Israel, and He also gave him the wisdom to build it. This is why Solomon wrote in Proverbs 19:8, "He that getteth wisdom loveth his own soul."

Therefore, don't grumble when you are passing through some difficult time—great promotion does not come easy. God might keep silent sometimes, but His silence does not mean He is not near to you.

Rather, say to those things troubling you, "I will surely overcome you. God will give me the victory. I will get the glory hereafter."

Whether in times of peace or trouble, remember that God is never far from you. He is knocking at the door—so open it for Him to come in. You can handle the problem properly with Him on your side. As we learn from Ephesians 3:20-21, Jesus is there to meet all of your needs.

"Unto him that is able to do exceeding abundantly above all that we ask or think, according to the power that worketh in us, unto him be glory."

Remember:

• God can take care of all the things that concern you.

• God can turn your present darkness into a great and bright light.

• God can turn your present condition around to something great and very beautiful.

• God can use this present problem of yours to bring about His good plans for your life.

• God can give you beauty for your ashes right now, and exchange a garment of praise for your spirit of heaviness.

• God can turn your present demotion to a great promotion, and establish you in a way that you've never dreamed of before.

• He can put you into a position that was denied to you earlier by men.

What He did for others He can also do for you—even in greater measure. Testimonies about His provision and deliverance can be found in every nation, and in every situation. Nothing is new before God.

Each obstacle that the Devil brings on your path, God uses as a stepping-stone for your progress and promotion. You will never be promoted until you become overqualified for your present position.

An overcoming spirit will surely always help you. If everyone around you is confused, don't participate in his or her bewilderment. If everything around you is falling apart, stay firmly in the will of God. When other things fail, the will of God for you will not fail. He will shine His face and power on you, and you will become a success.

 Don't focus and ruminate upon your obstacles—whatever the terrible situation that has harassed you. Rather, seek out a better alternative in Christ Jesus by expressing your trust in Him. You may have lost something important in life. However, it is useless to sit down and discuss it—lamenting and weeping over it—because that does not produce any beneficial results. Rather, rise up and find something positive to do that will glorify God. He can restore your loss or provide something more excellent.

There is no circumstance that can befall you that God cannot change. God always provides a way for you. When it seems as if the Devil has closed every available avenue for you, God will provide another way and you will experience the unending pleasure of God's goodness. God's plan is to move you from a less comfortable, less spiritually mature place to a more comfortable place where you are closer to Him. Sometimes that comes in the form of problems.

Your focus should be on the kingdom ahead—and the joy and glory expected therein. The present tribulation from adversaries should pose no distraction to you, because you are already overcoming through Christ Jesus. Every provision is already in place for your victory and success.

- Noah had tribulations, setbacks, and adversaries—yet he survived the flood.
- Sarah was barren and too elderly to give Abraham an heir—yet she conceived and bore a child against all odds and medical predictions.
- Joseph appeared forever doomed to prison—yet became the prime minister of Egypt.
- The nation of Israel had enormous odds against it in the wilderness—yet they conquered the Promised Land.

• David had great tribulations and was pursued by the jealous King Saul—yet he received the throne he'd been promised.

• Daniel had dangerous adversaries in a foreign land—yet he came out even more highly respected.

• The apostles had many enemies—yet the gospel was still preached and souls were won to the Lord Jesus Christ.

Have you identified the joy beyond your tribulations? Press on, keep the faith, cling to hope, and God will surely grant your expectations.

Hard work is very necessary and commendable, but Deuteronomy 8:18 says that promotion and wealth come only through the Lord God. All of your provisions are from Him.

In any particular situation, the discovery of God's plan and purpose for your life is called *vision*. Vision is generally unfolded in phases, and you cannot arrive at your glorious destiny until you discover it and work wholeheartedly at it. When you are driven by godly vision, you will not fall. Rather, you will excel and triumph in life and in all that you do.

Working with vision can transform an ordinary person into an extraordinary servant of God. However, you must be driven by godly vision and not by ambition. There is no shortcut to excellence, but the shortest and easiest way out of frustration is to abide in God's plan for your life.

"No temptation has overtaken you except such as is common to man; but God is faithful, who will not allow you to be tempted beyond what you are able, but with the temptation will also make the way of escape, that you may be able to bear it" (1 Corinthians 10:13 NKJV).

The stirring of the nest will not always be comfortable, but the reasons are right and the purposes are achievable.

 He that is with you will ensure your success. With God, you can and will do it right. Equip yourself with the actual knowledge of what the Devil is looking for in your life and resist it vehemently with prayers and with positive actions towards an expected goal. Christ Jesus told us in John 10:10 that, the Devil comes only to kill, to steal, and to destroy—but that He came to give us abundant life.

Check out people who have experienced similar problems as you face now, how they escaped, how and why it sank others, and how others—despite the same trouble—came out of it and rose up so high thereafter. Compare them with the standards of God and make your decisions based on God's Word and He will help you and give you grace. He told Paul, "My grace is sufficient for you" (2 Corinthians 12:9 NIV).

Chapter 3
In Nothing Be Terrified

We are in a wonderful time for great testimonies about the goodness of God because of the death and resurrection of our Lord Jesus Christ. He paid the ultimate price for us all on the cross.

There were testimonies before Christ, and there have been testimonies after Christ—and there will continue to be testimonies until the second coming of Christ Jesus. Yet, we are still waiting for the time of the greatest testimony ever spoken in the history of mankind—the testimony of the resurrection of the saints and the rapture of all believers.

Today, all of these great testimonies should challenge us to act confidently—knowing we have a good and caring Father, who will never fail us. His promises are forever true. He values us greatly. In fact, Matthew 10:29-31 reveals our worth before our God, "Are not two sparrows sold for a copper coin? And not one of them falls to the ground apart from your Father's will. But the very hairs of your head are all numbered. Do not fear therefore; you are of more value than many sparrows."

You are very important before your Father who is in heaven. He is ready to take you to the heights of abundant life if you will simply do His will.

These are some testimonies about Him from times past:

- He moved Abraham from his village to a great land

 that flowed with milk and honey, and made him the father of a very great nation.

- He moved Sarah from barrenness to motherhood.
- He moved Jabez from pain to joy and prosperity.
- He moved David from keeping sheep in a field, to the palace where he became the king.
- He moved Nehemiah from being the servant of a king, to becoming the rebuilder of Israel and the leader of his people.
- He moved Job from suffering to a greater and more honorable prosperity.
- He moved Joseph from prison to the office of prime minister of Egypt.
- He moved Daniel from slavery to the head of the region he dwelled in.
- He moved Peter from the fishing boat to the mission field to become an apostolic leader.
- He moved Matthew from being a tax collector to becoming a kingdom preacher.
- He moved Luke from being a healer of bodies to becoming a healer of souls through Jesus Christ.
- He moved Paul from being a legal advocate to being a kingdom advocate.

Has He promised you? He will do it. God alone can change destinies. Your time for change has come as well.

Brethren, grace is available to move you to a great position. Do not be afraid of that which befalls you today. Hold on to that unseen and mighty hand of God. Know that the only thing the Devil can produce is unfounded terror.

In all of the above cases, there was a strong, invisible

hand with them in the days of their trials—that was the hand of the Almighty God. That same hand is with you. Philippians 1:28 (NKJV) admonishes, "[Be] not in any way terrified by your adversaries, which is to them a proof of perdition, but to you of salvation, and that from God."

God expects us to be fully aware of the Devil's antics and completely prepared for him. We should be on guard, as 2 Corinthians 2:11 states, "Lest Satan should get an advantage of us: for we are not ignorant of his devices." There is an abundance of evidence in the Bible that informs us of the Devil and his activities (Job 1:7-12; 2:3-8).

I want to assure you that the gospel of Jesus Christ—the author of our salvation—is true and very effective in all things and in all ways. He is always defending us—we who have been bought with His blood—against all the works of our adversaries. The evidence of His blood can never be erased. He is ever ready to establish us by His grace. Your value before God appreciates each day as you walk with Him. And He promises to deliver you and lift you up whenever you encounter the powers of darkness.

The apostle Paul, in Philippians 1:27, talked about our conduct in all things and advised that we should maintain a good relationship with our Maker and with others—having one spirit, one mind, and one faith in Christ Jesus, and striving to prove the gospel true and very effective.

In 2 Timothy 4:14-18 (NKJV), Paul recounts his experience against wicked people and what ensued.

Alexander the coppersmith did me much harm. May the Lord repay him according to his works. You also must beware of him, for he has greatly resisted our words. At my first defense no one stood with me, but all forsook me. May it not be charged against them. But the Lord stood with me and strengthened me, so that the message might be preached fully through me, and that all the Gentiles might hear. Also I was delivered out of the mouth of the lion. And the Lord will deliver me from every evil work and preserve me for His heavenly kingdom. To Him be glory forever and ever. Amen!

Our adversaries will always try to terrify us, but our victory is completely assured in Him. The adversaries will try to make us fail, but we will not.

The terrifying works of the Devil come in several ways. His intention is to destroy our faith and our continuing trust in our Lord Jesus Christ, in order to take us captive. He does this through fear, sadness, low self-esteem, an unproductive and slothful life, failures—the list goes on.

Your purpose may have been delayed, damaged, changed, or rendered ineffective by the attacks of the Enemy; but never drop your vision for any reason. Your vision is your future. Remember that Job's friends and wife rejected him. Loneliness, suffering, and distress temporarily took over his life, but he had a very beautiful and enviable end (Job 42:10).

In 2 Corinthians 4:8-11 (NKJV), Paul explained,

We are hard-pressed on every side, yet not crushed; we are perplexed, but not in despair; persecuted, but not forsaken; struck down, but not destroyed—always carrying about in the body the dying of the Lord Jesus, that the life of Jesus also may be manifested in our body. For we who live are always delivered to death for Jesus' sake, that the life of Jesus also may be manifested in our mortal flesh.

The Devil attempts to leave his mark on all of his victims. But God does the extraordinary by washing us up and leaving behind His beauty. As Isaiah 61:1,3 testifies:

The Spirit of the Lord God is upon me; because the Lord hath anointed me to preach good tidings unto the meek; he hath sent me to bind up the brokenhearted, to proclaim liberty to the captives, and the opening of the prison to them that are bound . . . To appoint unto them that mourn in Zion, to give unto them beauty for ashes, the oil of joy for mourning, the garment of praise for the spirit of heaviness; that they might be called trees of righteousness, the planting of the Lord, that he might be glorified.

1. Fear

Fear is the emotion that you experience when you are in danger. However, fear is an offence against Christianity, because it hinders our testimonies and stops us from achieving greater things in life. Fear keeps us in a state of perpetual complaining—turning our attention from tomorrow to yesterday. With fear, you are always a day behind, living permanently in your past.

The Devil attacks Christians in many ways, seeking to generate fear in them. Fears of the known and of the unknown, and doubts about the efficacy of the Word of God and its saving power. This is because fear will stop us from going forward in every area of life through dark thoughts, which will cloud our thinking.

However, we know that the only sure weapon against fear is the Word of God. Psalm 119:105 (NIV) assure us, "Your word is a lamp to my feet and a light to my path."

 Through the light of the Word, we can escape every trap of the spirit of fear, because it illuminates the dark in the spiritual and physical realms. As we walk in the directions of the Word of God, we are bound to have success and achieve great progress.

God is not silent concerning our everyday predicaments. Rather than fear the adversary, fear God, worship Him, and keep your faith in Him alive. Don't forget that fear is a spirit, and that the gift of God is love—not fear. "God has not given us a spirit of fear, but of power and of love and of a sound mind" (2 Timothy 1:7).

The true, mature Christian keeps his expectation in God's promises alive until they are made manifest. "Surely he will never be shaken; the righteous will be in everlasting remembrance. He will not be afraid of evil tidings; His heart is steadfast, trusting in the Lord. His heart is established; He will not be afraid, until he sees his desire upon his enemies" (Psalm 112:6-8).

2. Sadness

Sadness is the state of being or feeling unhappy, regardless of what you are doing. The result of sadness is better imagined than experienced—it breeds disaffection, rejection, complaining, discouragement, contention, criticism, doubt, hatred, misplaced aggression, and it kills a person's vision.

We vehemently need to stand against all the plans and purposes of the Devil. Never allow the Devil to replace your joy with anything else. Cling to the joy Christ Jesus has given to you. Romans 8:37 assure you that you are more than conqueror through Christ Jesus.

This is because of God's provision in 1 Corinthians

10:13 (NKJV), "No temptation has overtaken you except such as is common to man; but God is faithful, who will not allow you to be tempted beyond what you are able, but with the temptation will also make the way of escape, that you may be able to bear it."

God is watching over you for good. His thoughts for you are higher than what the Devil can ever imagine or could hope to thwart. Therefore, rather than give in to sadness, seek the presence of the Lord. In His presence is fullness of joy and in His right hand are pleasures forevermore.

Today, the body of Christ—the church—and many Christian homes are suffering from serious, satanically inflicted sadness. It has stopped many from occupying their rightful positions in life. The Devil has left many lives broken with sadness through destructive relationships, divorce, drugs, drunkenness, financial failures, unfulfilled promises, delayed dreams, and harmful ambitions.

No one is exempt from the Enemy's attacks, but we can overcome them all individually and collectively. Isaiah 55:12-13 (NKJV) tells of your portion in Him,

> You shall go out with joy, and be led out with peace; the mountains and the hills shall break forth into singing before you, and all the trees of the field shall clap their hands. Instead of the thorn shall come up the cypress tree, and instead of the brier shall come up the myrtle tree; and it shall be to the Lord for a name, for an everlasting sign that shall not be cut off.

There is no crown for anyone from the Devil but a scar. Resist all attempts of the Devil to implant sadness in you by beginning with prayer. However, you must act fast. Claim the promise of 2 Corinthians 12:9 (NKJV), "He said to me,

 'My grace is sufficient for you, for My strength is made perfect in weakness.'"

Also, do not neglect fellowship with other believers. Share in the joy and testimonies of others. Look to God for your blessings always.

"Looking unto Jesus the author and finisher of our faith; who for the joy that was set before him endured the cross, despising the shame, and is set down at the right hand of the throne of God" (Hebrews 12:2).

3. Low self-esteem

Low self-esteem means feeling inferior, having a guilty conscience, condemning oneself, or deeming oneself incapable of doing anything good because of past experiences. This satanic method is very common to humanity, and it cuts across age, race, and gender barriers—including ministers.

Low self-esteem usually comes when you turn your focus from trusting God to trusting yourself. Know that you cannot deliver yourself, despite the skills and knowledge that you may possess. Only God, through Jesus Christ, can deliver and set you free.

When Jesus contemplated the weight of our sins at the garden of Gethsemane, He cried out to the Father saying, "If thou be willing, remove this cup from me: nevertheless not my will, but thine, be done" (Luke 22:42). When He considered the great price He would have to pay for us, the only thing He could do was pray to the Father—He neither looked to Himself, nor to any man. Thank God, Jesus never lost His focus on God the Father in any way.

How many of us are busy crying to others or focusing on ourselves. Despite the pains inflicted on you by the

adversary, never lose your focus on the Lord Jesus Christ.
He alone can bring everlasting relief.

Moses also suffered from the cruelty of adversaries from birth. Yet God never left him (Exodus 3:11-4:13). God was with Moses all the days of his life.

God gave Joshua the following advice before he faced the adversaries in Canaan. The counsel found in Joshua 1:7-8 (NKJV) guided him all the days of his life, and it is given to you as well.

Be strong and very courageous, that you may observe to do according to all the law which Moses My servant commanded you; do not turn from it to the right hand or to the left, that you may prosper wherever you go. This Book of the Law shall not depart from your mouth, but you shall meditate in it day and night, that you may observe to do according to all that is written in it. For then you will make your way prosperous, and then you will have good success.

This is your reward—success and victory. Your determination to go forward can pull down all the walls of low self-esteem. David moved with determination and great confidence in God, and he was able to overcome the mighty Goliath. Therefore, do not allow the devices or words of the adversary to determine your attitude, because it will leave you very miserable and confused. Rather, be moved by the Word of God.

Every day, God gives you a word that is sure to make your day a success. Live in it, walk in it, meditate on it, talk about it, be molded by it, and it will certainly make your life very beautiful. Every grace is available for you to overcome and become very successful.

As Jeremiah 1:7-8 says, "The Lord said to me: 'Do not

 say, "I am a youth," for you shall go to all to whom I send you, and whatever I command you, you shall speak. Do not be afraid of their faces, for I am with you to deliver you.'"

4. Fruitlessness

Many have become unproductive—not because they want to remain that way, but because of forces higher than themselves. They work so hard and put in so much, yet their harvest is always lean.

The adversary is pulling down many servants of God—great and small alike. Some find the path to recovery, while others are bound by fruitlessness—their great dreams, investments, homes, families, and relationships crumbling daily. We cannot afford to wait until we become useless to fight the adversary. We must be fruitful through Christ Jesus.

In Psalm 23:4-6, David said,

> Yea, though I walk through the valley of the shadow of death, I will fear no evil: for thou art with me; thy rod and thy staff they comfort me. Thou preparest a table before me in the presence of mine enemies: thou anointest my head with oil; my cup runneth over. Surely goodness and mercy shall follow me all the days of my life: and I will dwell in the house of the Lord forever.

And remember what David said in Psalm 78:72, "[God] shepherded them according to the integrity of his heart, and guided them by the skillfulness of his hands." God furnished a table in the wilderness for them during the forty years that they wandered. And He faithfully led them into the Promised Land.

God can turn your fortune today. He can restore you

beyond your greatest imaginations. He can take you to the Promised Land as well. The year of your deliverance has come.

"I will restore to you the years that the swarming locust has eaten, the crawling locust, the consuming locust, and the chewing locust, my great army which I sent among you" (Joel 2:25).

5. Failure

Failure is a general lack of success. The adversary uses failure as a tool to stop and discourage you. However, your present or past failures should not prevent you from going forward because there is every hope that you can be successful again. Proverbs 24:16 reminds us, "Though a righteous man falls seven times, he rises again." There is every possibility for you to rise up again and achieve your goals.

Many have changed churches, methods of worship, spouses, their names, and have even run away from home because of their failures. Truly brethren, God has not changed and His Word will never change. *Discover His word for your life and stand on it. All other things are but sinking sand.*

David, narrating his life story, said, "I waited patiently for the Lord; he turned to me and heard my cry. He lifted me out of the slimy pit, out of the mud and mire; he set my feet on a rock and gave me a firm place to stand" (Psalm 40:2 NIV). Rather than running, he trusted in the Lord. And God rewarded David by establishing him.

Our adversary has mapped out several things on our path to distract us from the true way of God and to deceive us into worshiping the Devil. Yet, Paul told us in Philippians 1:28, "In nothing [be] affrighted by the adversaries." This is because Paul knew that God has an everlasting love for all of His children.

God is still in love with you, despite what the adversary is doing. His love for you is never shaken by any of the things you are facing. Nothing can separate you from the Savior you trust—not even the adversary (Romans 8:35-39).

Many righteous people are having a tough time, while the unrighteous appear to have it easy. We are tempted to question our faith and even the existence of our God. However, God is impartial in His judgment, and He expects us to be impartial as well. He made the sun to shine on both the good and the evil, and sends rain both to the just and the unjust. All will be judged, so it is best to trust and obey Him.

Being attacked by these adversaries does not bring you any condemnation or rejection from God. Deuteronomy 19:15 (NKJV) says, "One witness shall not rise against a man concerning any iniquity or any sin that he commits; by the mouth of two or three witnesses the matter shall be established."

However, your action—when it is negative and sinful—brings the condemnation and subsequent rejection by God. "The person who turns to mediums and familiar spirits, to prostitute himself with them, I will set My face against that person and cut him off from his people" (Leviticus 20:6 NKJV).

Temptation—in itself—is not sin. But yielding to it is. Therefore, refrain from all forms of sin. Hold on to your God in faith. He alone knows all things—no one else can be compared to Him. He alone knows all about you and your destiny—and can provide for it sufficiently. He will give you the victory—so look up and expect real victory in Jesus' name.

Chapter 4
Heroes of Faith: A Study of Hebrews 11

Faith is a primary requirement for overcoming all the works of the adversary and for fulfilling all that we are destined to be in this life. Hebrews 11 is dedicated to the heroes of the Bible who had such remarkable faith. They all passed through great difficulties, yet they held on to their faith in God. They were people like us today, with great challenges and difficulties each day. Yet, their difficulties gave way for their victories because of how they applied their faith on a daily basis to those issues they faced. They are living proof that you can triumph over the threats of the adversary with faith in the living God. I will also want to add that working in faith will require the physical display of our trust in the Almighty God. It is an everyday living practice.

Hebrews 11:1 begins with the definition of faith. "Faith is the substance of things hoped for, the evidence of things not seen." If we ask in faith, we will also receive in faith. Therefore, whatever your need, ask God for it in faith. And though it may take a while to appear, continue to trust in God's ability to provide it for you. You will surely obtain what you hope for, just as the heroes of old did.

Faith, then, is the undying hope in God's ability to answer you and provide for you through Christ Jesus our

 Lord. As Jeremiah 17:7-8 promises,

Blessed is the man who trusts in the Lord, and whose hope is the Lord. For he shall be like a tree planted by the waters, which spreads out its roots by the river, and will not fear when heat comes; but its leaf will be green, and will not be anxious in the year of drought, nor will cease from yielding fruit.

The result of this undying faith in God is freshness, fruitfulness, and protection from every form of onslaught. 1 Corinthians 13:13 states, "These three remain: faith, hope and love." Therefore, we should develop an abiding faith, an enduring hope, and an unshakeable love.

In Hebrews 11:3 we learn, "The world was framed by the word of God, so that things which are seen were not made of things which do appear." God made the world with His words—not from things seen, but from things that did not yet exist. This is the basis of the great faith we are encouraged to emulate. If God created so much from nothing, then He can certainly help us. We can have faith and not fear failure.

Hebrews 11:4 (NIV) recounts an example of such faith. "Abel offered God a better sacrifice than Cain did. By faith he was commended as a righteous man, when God spoke well of his offerings. And by faith he still speaks, even though he is dead." Because of his faith, Abel pleased God with his offering. He suffered persecution, and was even killed because of his righteousness. Yet his testimony endures. Abel's kind of faith does not die—it speaks to us and encourages us in times of great problems. If we seek to please God, we must act in faith—because faith is the light that makes the righteous shine.

As we find in Hebrews 11:5 (NKJV), Enoch shone with such faith as well. "Enoch was taken away so that he did not see death, 'and was not found, because God had taken him'; for before he was taken he had this testimony, that he pleased God." Faith was all that Enoch needed to escape death. You also can escape your present calamities through faith as well.

However, just as faith pleases God, faithlessness displeases Him. Hebrews 11:6 teaches us, "Without faith it is impossible to please him: for he that cometh to God must believe that he is, and that he is a rewarder of them that diligently seek him." Faith requires diligent action. We must respond to the Word of God and allow it to increase our faith and guide our dealings.

Hebrews 11:7 (NIV) tells us, "Noah, when warned about things not yet seen, in holy fear built an ark to save his family." Noah believed God and acted upon His Word—point by point. Men mocked him, but when the flood came, he was able to survive with his family. His faith led him to a glorious end.

As did Abraham's faith. Hebrews 11:8-12 recounts how Abraham became a source of blessing to the whole world. By faith, Abraham became the father of a mighty nation, despite being childless for 99 years. Sarah, Abraham's wife, was 89 years old when she received the strength to conceive—even though she was well past the age of conception. They both lived out what they believed about their Lord, and He blessed them for it.

Obedience enhances and reinforces our trust in God. We come to understand that time and circumstances are in God's hands. He can turn our world around for good at any moment—so we trust Him in every moment.

That was the spirit behind the success and subsequent victory, deliverance, and restoration of Job. Job said, "Though He slay me, yet will I trust in Him, but I will maintain mine own ways before him" (Job 13:15). It is this spirit of absolute hope in God that guides us to such a beautiful testimony.

In fact, Abraham, Noah, and Job all had faith that continues to outlive them. It can give you a wonderful testimony that will outlive you as well.

Therefore, do not be terrified about anything. As Hebrews 11:17-19 teaches, Abraham was tested when God asked him to sacrifice his son Isaac. Without trepidation, he moved with great faith and hope that God would restore his child back to life. And God truly delivered Isaac and greatly rewarded Abraham for his faithfulness and obedience.

Hebrews 11:23 continues with the story of Moses, who was saved despite the death sentence placed upon all newborn male children in Egypt during his time. "Moses, when he was born, was hid three months of his parents, because they saw he was a proper child; and they were not afraid of the king's commandment." The death sentence did not deter his parents from keeping their son because they trusted in God.

Go ahead and obey every word of God for you despite the circumstances. Just as God hid Moses and his parents from all forms of persecutions, He will cover and protect you.

The product of this faith was that Moses became a great man in the land of Israel. Hebrews 11:25-26 (NKJV) testifies, "Choosing rather to suffer affliction with the people of God than to enjoy the passing pleasures of sin, esteeming the reproach of Christ greater riches than the treasures in

Egypt; [Moses] looked to the reward." Moses preferred spiritual benefits to temporal ones. He preferred to be identified with the Israelites instead of the Egyptians, and God honored his decision. While spiritual blessings often result in positive physical benefits, physical blessings usually do not lead to spiritual benefits. Therefore, Moses was wise and focused on what was most important.

Hope and faith in God can move you to great victory in life every day. By faith, you can achieve wonderful things and overcome evil. Yet, faith requires time—sometimes many years. Still, in the end, faith speaks beauty into your life and gives you great advantages. These advantages surely outweigh the time you spend waiting for your victory.

Faith in God's promises parted the Red Sea, brought down the wall of Jericho, and delivered Rehab and her family from death. Faith subdued nations, stopped evil tongues, brought righteousness and salvation, and overcame great adversaries. The miraculous results of faith can be experienced in our time once again. Through faith, you can obtain a good report for yourself; so let your faith speak to all of the situations you are facing right now.

I am a living witness of the great ministry of faith. If not for the grace of God and His unmerited miracles in my life, I would not have been alive today or be a preacher of the gospel of Christ Jesus.

The Devil tried on three different occasions to stop me from speaking fluently. I remember when I was a child and still growing teeth, I had an unusual experience. Instead of my baby teeth falling out in order for the adult teeth to grow, they rather grew inside my mouth—towards my nose. Though they weren't causing any pain, one morning I woke up with very sore teeth. By the evening of the same day, those baby teeth fell out without any medication—and the new adult teeth immediately took their places. Since then, I haven't experienced any pain. Imagine what would have happened if those baby teeth—which measured about one and a half centimeters when they came out—had pierced my nose!

The second obstacle was my stuttering. It was so severe that I always avoided meeting and talking with people—even family members. I quite remember receiving a beating from my mother the day I was talking with her about my dad. When I could not pronounce, "Dad," after several tries, I managed to say, "That man." That was an insult on his person that I never intended. To my surprise, I found myself set free from my stuttering problem the day that I was asked to read a Bible in the church—despite my attempts to avoid doing it.

The last attempt to stop me from speaking was in 1997. While rushing to get some financial things settled, and then running back to the church for a midweek preaching appointment, the bus I was riding in had an accident. No one had any serious injuries, and I had no physical wounds or pains. However, after three days, I discovered that I was unable to move my jaw or to chew anything. Despite my inability to open my mouth, my dentist could not identify what was wrong. An X-ray was recommended, and it revealed that my maxillary bone—the bone that holds the lower and upper jaws together—was broken.

Two options were recommended with severe conditions. First, I could have plastic surgery, but there was only a one in ten chance of survival and having a normal life thereafter. My second option was to have my upper and lower jaws sewn together for about six weeks to allow for an unshaken physical contact. This meant that I could not use my teeth, and I feared not being able to eat throughout that period though I have been used to long fasting before that period. I chose the second option, and after three weeks of surviving solely on fluids without medication, I asked for the stitches to be removed. By His grace, I was healed. Since then, I have experienced no such pains again.

This is just one of my testimonies of faith. Through faith in the blood of Jesus Christ, the angels prevailed against the Devil.

You will also prevail in Jesus' name. Mountain-moving Christians are faith-based Christians. We know from James 2:17, "Faith, if it hath not works, is dead." Do you want to move higher in the things of God? Would you like to develop your faith as you grow in grace each day? The apostles of old asked Jesus to increase their faith, and we need to pray such prayers today, and wait with patience to continue on the path He has chosen to lead us in for the enhancement of our faith. In the faith path you walk in, you don't choose the method or size or situation—God decides and you follow. Be armed with the assurance that He is right there to see you through.

Faith in Christ Jesus overcomes fear, brings miracles, and restores life and hope. The woman with the issue of blood, moved by faith, touched Jesus, and He brought her healing. Jairus, the synagogue ruler had his 12-year-old daughter raised from dead through faith (Mark 5:21-42).

Chapter 5
Our Defense

The kingdom of heaven is as real as the earth we live on today. So are the kingdom and the power of darkness. All forms of evil emanate from the Enemy's dark realm.

Through a revelation, I was shown that I faced a band of adversaries from the kingdom of darkness. I had not realized they were there, nor could I identify my enemies in the physical realm. To this day, I do not know all of the plans and accusations they formed against me. All I know is that they were evil and meant to do evil against me.

I was taken to a house that looked like a clubhouse. It was so dark inside that I could not identify any person next to me. All I could hear were the sounds of drums and wild music. All along I could sense the presence of the Lord within me, but was unable to say a word.

I was then taken to a corner of a large, dark room. I heard the mumble of an assembly, but their discussions were in such low tones that I could not hear them properly. Then, a high seat was prepared for the leader of the group. When it was time for the leader to come into the room, the music from the drums was amplified and human traffic into the room increased. The leader came in and walked straight to his seat—ready to discuss the matter of the day.

Immediately, I was called up to face my charges. Standing before the leader, the deep darkness in the room was suddenly broken by a bright light that unexpectedly appeared in the room. I did not know where the light came from, but it lit up the entire room and threw everyone into great confusion. Everyone ran out—which left me standing alone.

I know that the light was Jesus Christ—and that He came to save me at that perilous moment. God gave me the victory over those dark, unseen adversaries. We know that every day we fight with unseen forces. But in all, Christ Jesus is right there with us (1 Corinthians 4:9-16; 2 Corinthians 6:3-10).

We all should know that the kingdom of darkness is like an army, broken into regiments—each with a commander and soldiers. Satan is its leader. "The great dragon was cast out, that old serpent, called the Devil, and Satan, which deceiveth the whole world: he was cast out into the earth, and his angels were cast out with him" (Revelation 12:9). These fallen angels—a third of all the angels in heaven—rebelled along with Satan and share his fate. They are Satan's subordinates, and have agents in various forms—which carry out the assignments of their masters at the various levels.

These are their categories according to apostle Paul in Ephesians 6:12, "We wrestle not against flesh and blood, but against principalities, against powers, against the rulers of the darkness of this world, against spiritual wickedness in high places."

Irrespective of their organizational names, wicked men hide under each of these categories to afflict men with all forms of evil. They allow themselves to be used for evil works.

We need to understand that there is no middle ground—you are either with Christ Jesus doing good, or you are with the Devil doing evil.

During my ordeal, I knew that Jesus Christ was my defense. He said "I am with you always, even unto the end of the world" (Matthew 28:20). He will always speak for us in all cases.

The word from the throne of grace is that He accepts all who come to Him in sincere repentance. The Lord Jesus Christ died for all—not one will be rejected who truly repents and accepts Him. In Christ Jesus, there are enough rooms for all of us. In John 14:2 we learn that He is not only making provisions for our souls, but also for our bodies. Jesus says, "In my Father's house are many mansions: if it were not so, I would have told you. I go to prepare a place for you.

You are very important to Him, and He is ready to revitalize you completely. In Mark 10:29-30, Jesus says,

Verily I say unto you, There is no man that hath left house, or brethren, or sisters, or father, or mother, or wife, or children, or lands, for my sake, and the gospel's, but he shall receive an hundredfold now in this time, houses, and brethren, and sisters, and mothers, and children, and lands, with persecutions; and in the world to come eternal life.

Note the plurals used in referring to material things such as houses and lands. Jesus is speaking of the things you possess now—in this present world.

John 8:36 (NKJV) testifies, "If the Son makes you free, you shall be free indeed." Jesus Christ has indeed freed us through all the sufferings He went through, culminating with His death on the cross. This was the price He paid for our salvation—His blood.

Salvation in itself is a defense. We can truly rely on it in times of adversity—knowing that our God will defend us, deliver us, and keep us strong now and forever. Salvation is a defensive wall against the powers of our adversaries. We are told of its many joyful benefits in Isaiah 26:1-4,

In that day shall this song be sung in the land of Judah; we have a strong city; salvation will God appoint for walls and bulwarks. Open ye the gates that the righteous nation, which keepeth the truth, may enter in. Thou wilt keep him in perfect peace, whose mind is stayed on thee: because he trusteth in thee. Trust ye in the Lord forever: for in the Lord Jehovah is everlasting strength

Jesus Christ is the Captain of our salvation, and only through Him are we made perfect (Luke 1:69; Acts 4:12; Hebrews 2:10). Our salvation is from the Lord.

The Result of Salvation

Salvation is the most valuable possession you've ever had—so you should consider it as such. Jesus said in Matthew 6:33 (NKJV), "Seek first the kingdom of God and His righteousness, and all these things shall be added to you." By *all these things,* Jesus means, He includes both material and spiritual blessings in your reward.

Salvation required such a high price that it should never be taken for granted. It is a heavenly seal upon your life, which God paid for with the blood of Jesus Christ—the highest form of divine sacrifice. Jesus Christ offered Himself at the prayer garden of Gethsemane, and gave Himself for torture on the cross at Calvary.

It is only through salvation that we can become God's beloved children. And God does not take our salvation lightly—He is ready to defend us anytime and anywhere just because we bear His heavenly seal. In Matthew 18:6-7 (NKJV) He says,

> Whoever causes one of these little ones who believe in Me to sin, it would be better for him if a millstone were hung around his neck, and he were drowned in the depth of the sea. Woe to the world because of offenses! For offenses must come, but woe to that man by whom the offense comes!

Salvation can only be gained through the following steps:

1. Believing in the Lord Jesus Christ.
2. Accepting Him as your only Lord and Savior.
3. Confessing your sins to Him alone, and asking Him to forgive you.
4. Thereafter having a continuous relationship with Him through prayer.
5. Having fellowship with other believers in worship and Bible study.

A genuine salvation will disengage you from sin, and from participating in the things and works of sin. It does not mean that you will not be tempted, because you will be. Temptation in itself is not sin. However, yielding to temptation is. Yet, God will still pardon you when you acknowledge it and call upon Him for forgiveness.

The Devil will always try to tempt the children of God—that is his goal and character. Jesus said in John 10:10 (NKJV), "The thief [the Devil] does not come except to steal, and to kill, and to destroy." But thanks to our God for making the Devil's time against us short. He will receive the appropriate judgment and punishment for troubling us.

With this in mind, Paul the apostle encouraged the Galatians not to be distracted. "I have confidence in you, in the Lord, that you will have no other mind; but he who troubles you shall bear his judgment, whoever he is" (Galatians 5:10 NKJV).

Because of salvation—because you bear the mark of our Lord Jesus Christ—you stand out from the crowd. And the Devil dreads the good you could do. He has no control over a person who bears Christ's mark.

To help the Israelites escape from slavery, God sent a plague of death to Egypt. Yet in order to spare His people, God told the Israelites to place the blood of a sacrificial lamb upon their doorposts. He comforted them with the promise, "When He sees the blood on the lintel and on the two doorposts, the Lord will pass over the door and not allow the destroyer to come into your houses to strike you" (Exodus 12:23 NKJV). Once the destroyer had decimated the Egyptians, the Israelites could safely escape into the wilderness.

Similarly, the mark of the Lamb must be on you to keep the Devil away. Christ's mark is seen and known by your daily conduct, your relationships with others, and your fellowship with God through obedience and worship.

Paul the apostle said, "From now on let no one trouble me, for I bear in my body the marks of the Lord Jesus" (Galatians 6:17 NKJV). Surely, a genuine salvation affects your entire lifestyle—including your conduct and speech.

Other Benefits of Salvation

Jesus Christ is the Author of our salvation, and all the

benefits that He enjoys are ours as well. There are several benefits, but for the sake of brevity, here are just a few—rest, peace, strength, defense, light, opportunities, victories, renewal, escape from condemnation, help, eternal life, direction, deliverance, miracles, and mercy. This is what the Word of God promises you after your salvation,

You shall go out with joy, and be led out with peace; the mountains and the hills shall break forth into singing before you, and all the trees of the field shall clap their hands. Instead of the thorn shall come up the cypress tree, and instead of the brier shall come up the myrtle tree; and it shall be to the Lord for a name, for an everlasting sign that shall not be cut off (Isaiah 55:12-13 NKJV).

Truly speaking, the world cannot and will never satisfy its own needs. Yet, God is able to meet every need according to His riches in glory in all generations. Therefore, it is up to faithful believers to make God's provision known to the world. This is why the world is in such great need of Christians. Despite what anyone says, the lost are indeed eager to eat of the fruit of your salvation—they just may not realize it is what they long for. Yet, you can affect your world for God in your generation by leading the lost to the One who can help them.

Hebrews 6:9 (NKJV) says, "Beloved, we are confident of better things concerning you, yes, things that accompany salvation, though we speak in this manner." This Scripture contains two strong phrases concerning your salvation: *confident of better things*, and *things that accompany*. These are powerful words, indeed. We all are expected to bring forth the fruit of salvation; therefore, let us discuss a few of the ones mentioned above.

1. Rest

Rest here is not the absence of trouble, sorrow, or worry. Rather, it is the assurance of a divine solution from God. Jesus Christ is our burden bearer (Isaiah 53:4-11). When He spoke about rest, Jesus referred to real spiritual, physical, emotional, and material comfort. Both rest in this life, and rest in the life to come. Consider Jesus' words in Matthew 11:27-29 (NKJV),

All things have been delivered to Me by My Father, and no one knows the Son except the Father. Nor does anyone know the Father except the Son, and the one to whom the Son wills to reveal Him. Come to Me, all you who labor and are heavy laden, and I will give you rest. Take My yoke upon you and learn from Me, for I am gentle and lowly in heart, and you will find rest for your souls.

In the verse above, Jesus Christ explains what He is capable of and gives the assurance of rest to anyone who will come to Him. You cannot give what you don't have. Yet, Jesus said, "All authority has been given to me in heaven and on earth" (Matthew 28:18 NKJV). God is able to do all things.

Your rest is in Jesus Christ—and you can receive it today. Rest from God will come to you, because it is embedded in your salvation and in following Jesus Christ. Rely upon Him alone and you will find relief through His healing, deliverance, guardianship, peace of mind, and blessings. Meditating on His words and actions guarantees your comfort and peace.

In Luke 5:1-11, Jesus gave the disciples rest by providing them with an enormous catch of fish—though they had toiled all night without success. He simply asked for their obedience. Simon responded, "Master, we've worked hard all night and haven't caught anything. But because you say so, I will let down the nets" (v. 5 NIV). That act of obedience opened the way for the Savior's blessing and rest.

Your day of provision is here as you begin to believe and act upon the Word of God. He gave rest to a man who was an invalid for 38 years by healing him (John 5:1-9). He brought peace to the disciples as they faced a great storm at sea (Matthew 8:23-27). The winds, the seas, the mountains, and all creatures obey Him. How about you?

2. Peace

Peace is defined as a situation or period of time in which there is no war or violence in a country or an area. The next level of rest is peace from God and peace with self, which results in a soundness of mind concerning all things. When you reach this stage you find that nothing moves your faith in God. He promises to give you inner peace and peace with others as you work daily with Him—the Prince of Peace, Jesus Christ. Look at the following Scripture passages:

"Lord thou wilt ordain peace for us" (Isaiah 26:12).

"Follow peace with all men, and holiness, without which no man shall see the Lord" (Hebrews 12:14).

The apostle Paul gave us the following recipe for peace in 2 Timothy 2:22-26:

A. Jesus Christ is the Prince of Peace, and when we accept Him, we receive the peace that He offers. Rejecting Him means rejecting peace entirely.

B. We must flee from all forms of lust—lust for money,

 wealth, power, material things, sexual immorality, and political influence.

C. We must follow after righteousness.

D. We must have absolute faith in God.

E. We must practice charity with a pure heart.

F. We must avoid all forms of foolishness as quickly as possible.

G. We must avoid strife with everyone.

H. We must practice gentleness, meekness, and patience, and teach others to do likewise.

Paul concluded by saying, "That they may recover themselves out of the snare of the devil, who are taken captive by him at his will" (v. 26). If we live as people of peace, others will escape the snares of the Devil, and will serve God as well. The entire world is in desperate need of the peace of God. We all need peace in our families, communities, and countries. And you know what? Jesus is that peace. He is the only true peace the world can trust.

Examine the following verses:

"God is not the author of confusion, but of peace, as in all churches of the saints" (1 Corinthians 14:33).

"The peace of God, which surpasses all understanding, will guard your hearts and minds through Christ Jesus" (Philippians 4:7 NKJV).

"These things I have spoken to you, that in Me you may have peace. In the world you will have tribulation; but be of good cheer, I have overcome the world" (John 16:33 NKJV).

God is not the author of confusion; so wherever there is confusion ask Him to bring wisdom and peace. However, the peace of God is beyond the understanding and deliberations of people—irrespective of the caliber, intelligence, or importance of the committee members. Only in God can we find true and lasting peace, and He is willing to give it to anyone who will acknowledge his or her need.

3. Strength

The strength of any man is not measured by his physical size, but by what is inside of him. Being physically muscular does not signify spiritual strength. In the following verses, King David discloses the secrets of his success as the monarch of Israel.

The Lord is my light and my salvation; whom shall I fear? The Lord is the strength of my life; of whom shall I be afraid? When the wicked, even mine enemies and my foes, came upon me to eat up my flesh, they stumbled and fell. Though an host should encamp against me, my heart shall not fear: though war should rise against me, in this will I be confident . . . . For in the time of trouble he shall hide me in his pavilion: in the secret of his tabernacle shall he hide me; he shall set me up upon a rock. And now shall mine head be lifted up above mine enemies round about me: therefore will I offer in his tabernacle sacrifices of joy; I will sing, yea, I will sing praises unto the Lord . . . . The Lord will give strength unto his people; the Lord will bless his people with peace (Psalm 27:1-3,5-6; 29:11).

The anointing from heaven gives you strength, power, light, and the grace to succeed. Without this anointing, you cannot do any exploit for God. Yet, when God anoints you, He also ensures that you will succeed, unless you go against His instructions like Samson did.

Jesus said, "The Spirit of the Lord is upon me, because

 he hath anointed me to preach the gospel to the poor; he hath sent me to heal the brokenhearted, to preach deliverance to the captives, and recovering of sight to the blind, to set at liberty them that are bruised, to preach the acceptable year of the Lord" (Luke 4:18-19). His were real exploits—as were those of others who loved and obeyed God.

- Joseph survived all the hardships of slavery and prison through the strength and grace of God.
- Moses endured all of the harassments by the people of Israel and wanderings through the wilderness by God's power.
- Joshua led the Israelites into Jericho through the strength of God.
- Gideon destroyed the altars of Baal and subdued the Midianites through God's might.
- David defeated Goliath by the strength of God in him.
- Daniel excelled in the land of captivity through God's grace and power.

The strength of God cancels out the foolishness and weakness in you. In fact, He chooses the foolish things of the world to confound the wise—so that His power might be seen in them.

When he was 85 years old, Caleb said this to Joshua,

> As yet I am as strong this day as on the day that Moses sent me; just as my strength was then, so now is my strength for war, both for going out and for coming in. Now therefore, give me this mountain of which the Lord spoke in that day; for you heard in that day how the Anakim were there, and that the cities were great and fortified. It may be

that the Lord will be with me, and I shall be able to drive them out as the Lord said (Joshua 14:11-12 NKJV).

When the strength of heaven is with you, age is no barrier. It is amazing what the people of old did in their time. Yet, the anointing of God is always accompanied by inner and outer strength. Those that wait upon the Lord always renew their strength daily. They are like eagles that never grow weary. The Word of God builds spiritual and physical strength in all who trust Him, and also builds their faith.

As Isaiah 55:11 promises, "So shall my word be that goeth forth out of my mouth: it shall not return unto me void, but it shall accomplish that which I please, and it shall prosper in the thing whereto I sent it."

As God's Word accomplishes its assignments, so will you—especially as you hold on to the Word. The Word will never fail, and you will not fail as long as you follow it. Do you need strength? Read the Word.

4. Defense

To be defended by God is to have great protection all around you. It is a defense that never fails—that which is everlasting. However, this type of protection is never merely physical. Horses and chariots may fail, but God never fails. The Bible says, "Some trust in chariots, and some in horses; but we will remember the name of the Lord our God. They have bowed down and fallen; but we have risen and stand upright" (Psalm 20:7-8 NKJV).

It also says, "Woe to those who go down to Egypt for help, and rely on horses, who trust in chariots because they are many, and in horsemen because they are very strong, but who do not look to the Holy One of Israel, nor seek the Lord!" (Isaiah 31:1 NKJV).

God's defense on behalf of the redeemed is complete and very strong. He will defend us in every aspect of life until the very end. All He requires from us is that we honor and obey Him. Therefore heed the words of Isaiah 31:5-7 (NKJV),

> "Like birds flying about, so will the Lord of hosts defend Jerusalem. Defending, He will also deliver it; passing over, He will preserve it." Return to Him against whom the children of Israel have deeply revolted. For in that day every man shall throw away his idols of silver and his idols of gold—sin, which your own hands have made for yourselves.

When you dwell in God's secret place, you abide under His shadow. Nothing can penetrate His shadow—those under its protection are quite safe. He will be your refuge and fortress, and He will deliver you from all forms of satanic snares and pestilence. He will surely keep you from falling (Psalm 91).

Under God's protection, you enjoy a superlative life and peace every day. You are also delivered from known and unknown foes, fears, and all forms of destruction. As Psalm 91:7,11 assures you, "A thousand may fall at your side, and ten thousand at your right hand; but it shall not come near you . . . . For He shall give His angels charge over you, to keep you in all your ways" (NKJV). Hallelujah!

At salvation, you received the protection of God and His angels because you were bought with a great price. You are too precious to Him to go undefended. All of the protective armor of heaven is at your disposal to overcome satanic onslaughts. "The weapons of [your] warfare are not carnal, but mighty through God to the pulling down of strong holds" (2 Corinthians 10:4). Amen.

5. Light

Light is all we need to make any breakthrough in life. Every invention can credit its origin to the light the inventor receives—either through the accumulation of knowledge or revelation. You cannot afford to work in darkness again. For when the Word of God entered into you, it did not only bring you salvation, but it also brought you into the light of God and all the things that He has kept in store for you.

As Matthew 5:14-16 (NKJV) teaches, "You are the light of the world. A city that is set on a hill cannot be hidden. Nor do they light a lamp and put it under a basket, but on a lamp stand, and it gives light to all who are in the house. Let your light so shine before men, that they may see your good works and glorify your Father in heaven."

Your level of success depends on the amount of light you receive. God has not placed any limitation on you. At salvation, all limits were removed, and you were given the freedom to excel (Isaiah 40:31). Therefore,

> Arise; shine for your light has come! And the glory of the Lord is risen upon you. For behold, the darkness shall cover the earth, and deep darkness the people; but the Lord will arise over you, and His glory will be seen upon you. The Gentiles shall come to your light, and kings to the brightness of your rising (Isaiah 60:1-3 NKJV).

Look at the following statement in Isaiah 62:1-4 (NKJV). It is from the Lord to you, and He wants you to hold on to it.

For Zion's sake I will not hold My peace, and for Jerusalem's sake I will not rest, until her righteousness goes forth as brightness, and her salvation as a lamp that burns. The Gentiles shall see your righteousness, and all kings your glory. You shall be called by a new name, which the mouth of the Lord will name. You shall also be a crown of glory in the hand of the Lord, and a royal diadem in the hand of your God. You shall no longer be termed Forsaken, nor shall your land any more be termed Desolate; but you shall be called Hephzibah, and your land Beulah; for the Lord delights in you, and your land shall be married.

Only light can expel the darkness in your life completely. And when all forms of darkness are out of your life, breakthroughs, successes, and a spirit of celebration will be manifested greatly in you. It is light that empowers, reveals, and distinguishes colors. No doubt you will burst into great celebration because of the light of God that you have received.

John 1:4-5 has this to say about the light we receive in Christ Jesus, "In him was life; and the life was the light of men. And the light shineth in darkness; and the darkness comprehended it not."

6. Open doors

Who could possibly bind you again, once Jesus Christ has opened all of the doors of captivity against you? For He has been given the key to your ultimate freedom. "The key of the house of David I will lay on his shoulder; so he shall open, and no one shall shut; and he shall shut, and no one shall open" (Isaiah 22:22 NKJV).

Jesus Christ only has the true key to life—to abundance, to blessings, and to good health. All other keys keep man in bondage and condemnation. Yet, Jesus Christ has opened the door for everyone that will call upon Him in truth and with a pure heart (Revelation 1:18).

Salvation means liberty from all satanic captivity. Therefore, arise and demand your right. Don't allow yourself to be held back again. "These things said He who is true, He who has the key of David, He who opens and no one shuts, and shuts and no one opens" (Revelation 3:7, author's rendering).

Psalm 107:15-16 laments (NKJV), "Oh, that men would give thanks to the Lord for His goodness, and for His wonderful works to the children of men! For He has broken the gates of bronze, and cut the bars of iron in two."

Jesus broke the gate of death against Lazarus, tore asunder the gate of legalism against the Israelites, and opened the gates of heaven for all of us who believe in Him to go in.

Isaiah 60:11-12 (NKJV) assures us that the gates of God's blessings are always open for all of His children. "Therefore your gates shall be open continually; they shall not be shut day or night, that men may bring to you the wealth of the Gentiles, and their kings in procession. For the nation and kingdom which will not serve you shall perish, and those nations shall be utterly ruined."

You will not be held back again by closed doors. Salvation gave you permanent access into the kingdom of God and all of His blessings. "And the gates of Hades shall not prevail against it "(Matthew 16:18 NKJV).

7. Victory

At salvation, not only did God open the door of heaven for you, He also gave you the victory over the Devil, his evil minions, and their wicked plans. God gave you the ability to triumph over sin and its destructive work—over self and the evil desires of the flesh. This He did through the charge, "Touch not mine anointed" (Psalm 105:15). Evil no longer has a right to harm you. We learn from Isaiah 25:8-10 (NKJV),

He will swallow up death forever, and the Lord God will wipe away tears from all faces; the rebuke of His people He will take away from all the earth; for the Lord has spoken. And it will be said in that day: "Behold, this is our God; we have waited for Him, and He will save us. This is the Lord; we have waited for Him; we will be glad and rejoice in His salvation." For on this mountain the hand of the Lord will rest, and Moab shall be trampled down under Him, as straw is trampled down for the refuse heap"

Victory is the stage in which one stands firm over the calamities of life and its difficulties. Once you are victorious, then the next level you experience is being lifted up—not only triumphing over obstacles, but actually using them as your stepping stones. "For whatever is born of God overcomes the world. And this is the victory that has overcome the world—our faith. Who is he who overcomes the world, but he who believes that Jesus is the Son of God" (1 John 5:4-5 NKJV).

Jesus Christ makes your victory sure through your ever-increasing faith and continuous belief in His Lordship. With Christ Jesus, your victory is quite sure, despite all the works of your adversaries.

8. Renewal

Renewal is necessary for every generation, and it can

only be achieved through Jesus Christ. Being born again means receiving a complete transformation in every area of your life. Jesus Christ is interested in everything that concerns you. That is why salvation is a total package of life transformation and a complete renewal of all things—including thoughts, words, and actions.

We are admonished in Romans 12:1-2,

> I beseech you therefore, brethren, by the mercies of God, that ye present your bodies a living sacrifice, holy, acceptable unto God, which is your reasonable service. And be not conformed to this world: but be ye transformed by the renewing of your mind, that ye may prove what is that good, and acceptable, and perfect, will of God.

This much-needed transformation begins in your heart, where the Spirit of God seeks to dwell and work through you. Your heart is very important to God because it is the gateway through which the Spirit of God can renew your mind. This results in the renewal of your total self—spirit, soul, and body. Once your heart and mind are renewed and brought into conformity with the things of God, your ideas, thoughts, imagination, vision, taste, and even language will become pure. This enables you to serve God and worship Him in truth and in spirit.

In 1 Timothy 4:12 (NKJV), Paul admonishes Timothy, "Be an example to the believers in word, in conduct, in love, in spirit, in faith, in purity." Purity is the product of salvation. Without Jesus Christ, you cannot achieve purity of mind and of the spirit.

9. Escape From All Condemnation

The Devil's goal is to bring condemnation—whether real

 or imagined—to Christians and non-believers alike. He does so through the evil devices of his agents—our adversaries. However, we must give thanks to God because He justifies us against all the charges of the Enemy. "The thief cometh not, but for to steal, and to kill, and to destroy: I am come that they might have life, and that they might have it more abundantly" (John 10:10).

The Devil brings temptations and troubles to Christians to make us sin and become filthy before our God who loves us. Yet, we know from Romans 8:1, "There is therefore now no condemnation to them which are in Christ Jesus." And Jesus said,

> Whosoever believeth in him should not perish, but have eternal life. . . . For God sent not his Son into the world to condemn the world; but that the world through him might be saved. He that believeth on him is not condemned: but he that believeth not is condemned already, because he hath not believed in the name of the only begotten Son of God (John 3:15,17-18).

If we believe in Him, He forgives our sin and removes all of our guilt. In John 8:11 (NKJV), Christ told the woman caught in the act of adultery, "Neither do I condemn you; go and sin no more." John 8:36 (NKJV) confirms, "If the Son makes you free, you shall be free indeed." Therefore, we should never believe the lies of the Enemy that we are still condemned, because we know he only wishes to bind us with the chords of shame—shame that has been permanently removed.

These are sure words from Jesus Christ to keep you in victory,

My sheep hear My voice, and I know them, and they follow Me. And I give them eternal life, and they shall never perish; neither shall anyone snatch them out of My hand. My Father, who has given them to Me, is greater than all; and no one is able to snatch them out of My Father's hand. I and My Father are one (John 10:27-30 NKJV).

It does not matter what trial you are passing through right now, His word to you is that nothing can snatch you out of His hands. He is protecting you, and His love for you has no end. Just as Daniel escaped the lion's den without injury, and Shadrach, Meshach, and Abednego escaped the burning fiery furnace without harm, you will escape also.

Thus says the Lord, who created you, O Jacob, and He who formed you, O Israel: "Fear not, for I have redeemed you; I have called you by your name; you are Mine. When you pass through the waters, I will be with you; and through the rivers, they shall not overflow you. When you walk through the fire, you shall not be burned, nor shall the flame scorch you. For I am the Lord your God, the Holy One of Israel, your Savior; I gave Egypt for your ransom, Ethiopia and Seba in your place" (Isaiah 43:1-3 NKJV).

10. Help

Everyone needs help. No person is completely self-sufficient—only God is. People fail, the weapons of war fail, and all human securities and defenses fail—but God will never fail. His help will lead you to His everlasting love, protection, success, and abundance.

In Isaiah 49:8 (NKJV) He promises, "In an acceptable time I have heard You, and in the day of salvation I have helped You; I will preserve You and give You as a covenant to the people, to restore the earth, to cause them to inherit the desolate heritages."

 The Bible also teaches:

• "God is our refuge and strength, a very present help in trouble. Therefore will not we fear, though the earth be removed, and though the mountains be carried into the midst of the sea" (Psalm 46:1-2).

• "Give us help from trouble: for vain is the help of man. Through God we shall do valiantly: for he it is that shall tread down our enemies" (Psalm 60:11-12).

• "Our help is in the name of the Lord, who made heaven and earth" (Psalm 124:8).

Neglecting the salvation that was freely given to us through Jesus Christ means rejecting its great and numerous benefits. As we are told in Hebrews 2:3, "How shall we escape, if we neglect so great salvation; which at the first began to be spoken by the Lord, and was confirmed unto us by them that heard him."

11. Mercy

Another great benefit of salvation is the outpouring of God's mercy upon us. The Bible confirms that all have sinned and gone astray, and fall short of God's glory. Yet, God still restores people to a right relationship with Himself through Christ Jesus. All Christians today are products of the love and mercy of God—not of any individual work.

His mercy brought us into His love, which resulted in our being forgiven, justified, and accepted. Without mercy, there is no love, there is no forgiveness, and there is no acceptance.

We received God's love and mercy when we accepted Jesus Christ as our Lord and Savior by faith—confessing our sins and forsaking them. God loves the whole world, but only shows mercy to those who trust Him and look to Him for grace. He demonstrated this to Noah, David, Matthew, and Paul.

He exhibited it to Moses as well when He said, "I will make all My goodness pass before you, and I will proclaim the name of the Lord before you. I will be gracious to whom I will be gracious, and I will have compassion on whom I will have compassion" (Exodus 33:19 NKJV).

The mercies of the Lord endure forever. David discovered this and proclaimed in Psalm 23:6, "Surely goodness and mercy shall follow me all the days of my life." This is a testimony for you as a child of God. The mercies of the Lord cannot be compared with anything else in the world. He is longsuffering and great in compassion (Numbers 14:18).

"Through the Lord's mercies we are not consumed, because His compassions fail not. They are new every morning; great is Your faithfulness" (Lamentation 3:22-23 NKJV).

Your growth in grace and holiness begins with the level of mercy you receive from God. "O Israel, hope in the Lord; for with the Lord there is mercy, and with Him is abundant redemption. And He shall redeem Israel from all his iniquities" (Psalm 130:7-8).

Chapter 6
Scriptural Assurance To Encourage Us

Your ability to receive anything from God is contingent upon your absolute belief in His words without any reservation. You have every reason to be victorious in all of your battles against the Devil. However, you can't afford to be a disgrace before our Lord. Our Lord Jesus Christ had victory—therefore, the apostles had victory, the angels had victory, and the church has had and continues to have victory. So everyone redeemed by the Lord Jesus Christ should have victory over the Devil and all his minions as well.

In 1 Corinthians 15:25,57-58 (NKJV), you are admonished to allow Jesus Christ to reign in and through you.

> He must reign till He has put all enemies under His feet. . . . Thanks be to God, who gives us the victory through our Lord Jesus Christ. Therefore, my beloved brethren, be steadfast, immovable, always abounding in the work of the Lord, knowing that your labor is not in vain in the Lord.

What makes you the beloved of the Lord is the indwelling of His Spirit in you. "If the Spirit of Him who raised Jesus from the dead dwells in you, He who raised Christ from the dead will also give life to your mortal bodies through His Spirit who dwells in you" (Romans 8:11 NKJV).

 The requirements for victorious living are:

1. Accepting Jesus Christ as your only Lord and Savior.
2. Keeping His instructions and a vibrant daily fellowship with Him.
3. Being steadfast in worship and in belief.
4. Being rooted and grounded in Him by studying the Bible and meditating on His Word.
5. Abounding in good works—in speech, in character, and in all truthfulness.
6. Having a continuous indwelling of the Holy Spirit and relying on His guidance and assistance every day.
7. Accepting and trusting in God's Word without hesitation.

The Devil will try to tempt you as often as possible. But with consistent faith and prayer, you will have victory over him because Jesus Christ did. The Word of God is very effective, if accepted without any reservations.

Some Topical Scriptures of Assurance

We should know and accept that Jesus Christ paid the price for our total victory in all things.

Surely he hath borne our grief, and carried our sorrows: yet we did esteem him stricken, smitten of God, and afflicted. But he was wounded for our transgressions, he was bruised for our iniquities: the chastisement of our peace was upon him; and with his stripes we are healed (Isaiah 53:4-5).

He that spared not his own Son, but delivered him up for us all, how shall he not with him also freely give us all things? (Romans 8:32)

Unto him that is able to do exceeding abundantly above all that we ask or think, according to the power that worketh in us (Ephesians 3:20).

The Bible declares that our daily ordeal with the Devil is a war, and it teaches us how to win the battle at every stage. The only place the Devil belongs in your life is under your feet—defeated and powerless. Do not permit him to dwell in any other place. Even now, you can send him where he belongs, and remind him that he will never be able to prevail against the Lord God.

Therefore, for encouragement, read the following selected passages carefully. Use them in your prayers and praises.

1. A promise to give you victory.

A thousand shall fall at thy side, and ten thousand at thy right hand; but it shall not come nigh thee. Only with thine eyes shalt thou behold and see the reward of the wicked. Because thou hast made the Lord, which is my refuge, even the most High, thy habitation; there shall no evil befall thee, neither shall any plague come nigh thy dwelling (Psalm 91:7-10).

2. Promises to lift you up.

Draw nigh to God, and he will draw nigh to you. Cleanse your hands, ye sinners; and purify your hearts, ye double minded. . . . Humble yourselves in the sight of the Lord, and he shall lift you up (James 4:8,10).

Casting all your care upon him; for he careth for you. . . .

 The God of all grace, who hath called us unto his eternal glory by Christ Jesus, after that ye have suffered a while, make you perfect, stablish, strengthen, settle you (1 Peter 5:7,10).

3. Promises for victory over satanic weapons.

Indeed they shall surely assemble, but not because of Me. Whoever assembles against you shall fall for your sake. "Behold, I have created the blacksmith who blows the coals in the fire, who brings forth an instrument for his work; and I have created the spoiler to destroy. No weapon formed against you shall prosper, and every tongue, which rises against you in judgment, you shall condemn. This is the heritage of the servants of the Lord, and their righteousness is from Me," says the Lord (Isaiah 54:15-17 NKJV).

The weapons of our warfare are not carnal but mighty in God for pulling down strongholds, casting down arguments and every high thing that exalts itself against the knowledge of God, bringing every thought into captivity to the obedience of Christ, and being ready to punish all disobedience when your obedience is fulfilled (2 Corinthians 10:4-6 NKJV).

He answered and said, Every plant, which my heavenly Father hath not planted, shall be rooted up (Matthew 15:13).

Jesus said to them, "Because of your unbelief; for assuredly, I say to you, if you have faith as a mustard seed, you will say to this mountain, 'Move from here to there,' and it will move; and nothing will be impossible for you" (Matthew 17:20 NKJV).

4. Promises for victory over sin.

He that committeth sin is of the devil; for the devil sinneth from the beginning. For this purpose the Son of God was manifested, that he might destroy the works of the devil. Whosoever is born of God doth not commit sin; for his seed remaineth in him: and he cannot sin, because he is born of God (1 John 3:8-9).

Whatsoever is born of God overcometh the world: and this is the victory that overcometh the world, even our faith. Who is he that overcometh the world, but he that believeth that Jesus is the Son of God? (1 John 5:4-5).

5. Promises for victory over Satan and his agents.

Moses said to the people, "Do not be afraid. Stand still, and see the salvation of the Lord, which He will accomplish for you today. For the Egyptians whom you see today, you shall see again no more forever. The Lord will fight for you, and you shall hold your peace" (Exodus 14:13-14 NKJV).

The Lord will cause your enemies who rise against you to be defeated before your face; they shall come out against you one way and flee before you seven ways (Deuteronomy 28:7 NKJV).

I will give you the keys of the kingdom of heaven, and whatever you bind on earth will be bound in heaven, and whatever you loose on earth will be loosed in heaven (Matthew 16:19 NKJV).

We do not wrestle against flesh and blood, but against

 principalities, against powers, against the rulers of the darkness of this age, against spiritual hosts of wickedness in the heavenly places. Therefore take up the whole armor of God, that you may be able to withstand in the evil day, and having done all, to stand (Ephesians 6:12-13 NKJV).

Read also Matthew 18:18-20; Luke 10:17-19; and Romans 8:37. You can have that victory.

6. Promises for victory over fear.

You shall not be afraid of the terror by night, nor of the arrow that flies by day, nor of the pestilence that walks in darkness, nor of the destruction that lays waste at noonday. A thousand may fall at your side, and ten thousand at your right hand; but it shall not come near you (Psalm 91:5-7 NKJV).

Say to those who are fearful-hearted, "Be strong, do not fear! Behold, your God will come with vengeance, with the recompense of God; He will come and save you" (Isaiah 35:4 NKJV).

"Do not be afraid of their faces, for I am with you to deliver you," says the Lord. . . . "They will fight against you, but they shall not prevail against you. For I am with you," says the Lord, "to deliver you" (Jeremiah 1:8,19 NKJV).

Fear not: for I am with thee (Isaiah 43:5).

7. Promises for victory over barrenness, sickness, and death.

There shall nothing cast their young, nor be barren, in thy land: the number of thy days I will fulfill (Exodus 23:26).

You shall be blessed above all peoples; there shall not be a male or female barren among you or among your livestock. And the Lord will take away from you all sickness, and will afflict you with none of the terrible diseases of Egypt, which you have known, but will lay them on all those who hate you (Deuteronomy 7:14-15 NKJV).

The righteous shall flourish like the palm tree: he shall grow like a cedar in Lebanon. Those that be planted in the house of the Lord shall flourish in the courts of our God. They shall still bring forth fruit in old age; they shall be fat and flourishing; to shew that the Lord is upright: he is my rock, and there is no unrighteousness in him (Psalm 92:12-15).

Remember what He did for Sarah and Hannah—He gave them the desires of their hearts. He will also do it for you (Genesis 21:1-7; 1 Samuel 2:1-10).

8. Assurance of deliverance from sickness.

These signs will follow those who believe: In My name they will cast out demons; they will speak with new tongues; they will take up serpents; and if they drink anything deadly, it will by no means hurt them; they will lay hands on the sick, and they will recover (Mark 16:17-18 NKJV).

It shall come to pass in that day that his burden will be taken away from your shoulder, and his yoke from your neck, and the yoke will be destroyed because of the anointing oil (Isaiah 10:27 NKJV).

"In that day," says the Lord of hosts, "the peg that is

 fastened in the secure place will be removed and be cut down and fall, and the burden that was on it will be cut off; for the Lord has spoken" (Isaiah 22:25 NKJV).

He sent from above, He took me; He drew me out of many waters. He delivered me from my strong enemy, from those who hated me, for they were too strong for me. They confronted me in the day of my calamity, but the Lord was my support. He also brought me out into a broad place; He delivered me because He delighted in me. (Psalm 18:16-19 NKJV).

"I will surely deliver you, and you shall not fall by the sword; but your life shall be as a prize to you, because you have put your trust in Me," says the Lord (Jeremiah 39:18 NKJV).

Read also Isaiah 43:1-7; John 8:36; Acts 16:18; and 2 Peter 2:9.

9. Assurance of His presence.

No man shall be able to stand before you all the days of your life; as I was with Moses, so I will be with you. I will not leave you nor forsake you (Joshua 1:5 NKJV).

The Lord said to Joshua, "This day I will begin to exalt you in the sight of all Israel, that they may know that, as I was with Moses, so I will be with you" (Joshua 3:7 NKJV).

When you pass through the waters, I will be with you; and through the rivers, they shall not overflow you. When you walk through the fire, you shall not be burned, nor shall the flame scorch you (Isaiah 43:2 NKJV).

"Teaching them to observe all things that I have commanded you; and lo, I am with you always, even to the end of the age" (Matthew 28:20 NKJV).

I will not leave you as orphans; I will come to you (John 14:18 NIV).

Let your conduct be without covetousness; be content with such things as you have. For He Himself has said, "I will never leave you nor forsake you" (Hebrews 13:5 NKJV).

I am persuaded, that neither death, nor life, nor angels, nor principalities, nor powers, nor things present, nor things to come, nor height, nor depth, nor any other creature, shall be able to separate us from the love of God, which is in Christ Jesus our Lord (Romans 8:38-39).

10. Promises of guidance.

I will instruct you and teach you in the way you should go; I will guide you with My eye (Psalm 32:8 NKJV).

This God is our God forever and ever: he will be our guide even unto death (Psalm 48:14).

Associate yourselves, O ye people, and ye shall be broken in pieces; and give ear, all ye of far countries: gird yourselves, and ye shall be broken in pieces; gird yourselves, and ye shall be broken in pieces. Take counsel together, and it shall come to nought; speak the word, and it shall not stand: for God is with us (Isaiah 8:9-10).

The Lord will guide you continually, and satisfy your soul in drought, and strengthen your bones; you shall be like a watered garden, and like a spring of water, whose waters do not fail (Isaiah 58:11 NKJV).

To give light to them that sit in darkness and in the shadow of death, to guide our feet into the way of peace (Luke 1:79).

However, when He, the Spirit of truth, has come, He will guide you into all truth; for He will not speak on His own authority, but whatever He hears He will speak; and He will tell you things to come (John 16:13 NKJV).

11. Promises to stand by His Word.

So shall my word be that goeth forth out of my mouth: it shall not return unto me void, but it shall accomplish that which I please, and it shall prosper in the thing whereto I sent it (Isaiah 55:11).

Heaven and earth shall pass away, but my words shall not pass away (Matthew 24:35).

There is power in every word of God you hear, speak, or meditate on. As you receive the Word, allow it to dwell in you and replay itself. Apply it appropriately to every situation in your life. Remember, the Word of God is God Himself. Don't wait until you are in trouble or have a problem before you run to the Word. Make it your daily food and you will experience blessings in all things every day.

Declare the Word and the situation will change. Stand on it until your testimony goes ahead of you. Faith makes the Word more effective in your life—faith makes prayer work. Always trust Him to fulfill His promises in your life—especially as you speak or pray in Jesus' name.

12. Promises to defend us.

In all these things we are more than conquerors t
him that loved us (Romans 8:37).

Their rock is not as our Rock, even our enemies themselves being judges (Deuteronomy 32:31).

Fear thou not; for I am with thee: be not dismayed; for I am thy God: I will strengthen thee; yea, I will help thee; yea, I will uphold thee with the right hand of my righteousness. Behold, all they that were incensed against thee shall be ashamed and confounded: they shall be as nothing; and they that strive with thee shall perish. Thou shalt seek them, and shalt not find them, even them that contended with thee: they that war against thee shall be as nothing, and as a thing of nought. For I the Lord thy God will hold thy right hand, saying unto thee, Fear not; I will help thee (Isaiah 41:10-13).

Submit yourselves therefore to God. Resist the devil, and he will flee from you. Draw nigh to God, and he will draw nigh to you. Cleanse your hands, ye sinners; and purify your hearts, ye double minded. . . . Humble yourselves in the sight of the Lord, and he shall lift you up (James 4:7-8,10).

The Lord shall cause thine enemies that rise up against thee to be smitten before thy face: they shall come out against thee one way, and flee before thee seven ways (Deuteronomy 28:7).

Read these promises about your health and healing: Exodus 23:25; Deuteronomy 7:15; Psalm 107:20; Jeremiah 30:17; Matthew 8:16; Mark 16:18; and 1 Peter 2:24.

Chapter 7
Something Must Give Way

For you to be successful, there must be a change. Everything is subject to change. However, for a desired change to take place, there must be a calculated applied force. Spiritual force must be utilized to enact a spiritual change, and physical force employed for a physical change. However, when a spiritual force holds a desired physical change back, you must apply another force to advance that desired change. That is the warfare prayer of Christendom.

Understand that spiritual weapons are more lethal than physical ones. "[They are] mighty through God to the pulling down of strong holds; casting down imaginations, and every high thing that exalteth itself against the knowledge of God, and bringing into captivity every thought to the obedience of Christ" (2 Corinthians 10:4-5). Spiritual weapons cannot be limited or hindered by physical forces.

The color or accessories of an automobile are immaterial—its brakes must be applied in order to bring it to a stop. Imagine a car without brakes. Even if it has the latest technological comforts; eventually, it will crash and kill its occupants.

You must apply your spiritual brakes to the activities of the Devil in order not to crash as well. Bad situations must be forced to change via spiritual means. You must confront them with faith in the name of Jesus Christ. However, you cannot correct or change something you are not willing to confront.

 A brother gave a testimony of how he was being harassed and buffeted every night in his dreams by overwhelmingly strong, unseen forces. Each night, he would go to bed with fear, and every morning he would wake up angry and upset by what he experienced in his sleep. The adversaries would force him to eat whatever they stuffed into his mouth, have sexual relations with people he could not identify, and oblige him to pay debts he never owed.

One day, he heard a message that roused his anger and gave him the courage to face this sad aspect of his life. He decided, "Enough is enough!"

The following night, after he had prepared all day with fasting and Scripture recitation. He stood against the powers that had been dominating his life. He confronted them with serious prayers, and God gave him a permanent and complete victory.

Anger rightly applied generates power, boldness, and energy which will result in your deliverance and liberation from the powers of the Devil. However, you will not change any bad situation until you set yourself against it and take a positive step to correct it. Anger can open the battlefield.

Anger revealed the power of Elijah's mantle to Elisha. Anger made Hannah to go to the temple of God for prayer instead of dining at home with her husband. Because of her sincere prayers, God opened her womb and Samuel the prophet was born. The Devil is afraid when you are angry against him.

David said in Psalm 23:5-6 (NKJV), "You prepare a table before me in the presence of my enemies; you anoint my head with oil; my cup runs over. Surely goodness and mercy shall follow me all the days of my life; and I will dwell in the house of the Lord forever." He was ready to stand up for his portion from God.

Note here that David's table was in the full view of his enemies, but God gave him the power to endure their scrutiny. Goodness and mercy were his companions throughout his life, and he vowed to dwell with God forever. David understood what God had created him for.

So will you, if you will do as David did. Therefore, rise up against all your opposition in faith. With God on your side, you will overcome them all.

I have witnessed many healings and I have seen God's divine deliverance in many hopeless situations. God is willing to work with you in your present situation, but He is not willing to share you with anyone else. He is a jealous God and a consuming fire (Exodus 34:14; Deuteronomy 4:25). So take this as a prophecy for you right now—someone or something must give way in order for you to have complete victory.

Definitely, two captains cannot steer the same ship at the same time. One must give way for the other. Likewise, you must be willing to say, "Behold, I have come to do Your will, O God" (Hebrews 10:9 NKJV). Scripture speaks to the fact that evil must give way for good, and the wicked must give way for the righteous. In order for the Lord Jesus Christ to reign in your life and circumstances, the Devil must be driven out.

Therefore, build up your faith for your battle against all of your wicked adversaries. Build up your holy faith and give supremacy in your everyday affairs to God. Identify the darkness that enslaves you, and command it to be gone.

You are set for promotion through the Lord who had given you victory. As Psalm 75:6-7 (NKJV) promises, "Exaltation comes neither from the east nor from the west nor from the south. But God is the Judge: He puts down one, and exalts another."

Twenty Six things that must give way for you!

1. No matter the void, gloominess, or darkness in your life—it must give way for the Word of God to be manifested in you. All darkness gives way when the light of heaven shines on you.

In the beginning God created the heaven and the earth. And the earth was without form, and void; and darkness was upon the face of the deep. And the Spirit of God moved upon the face of the waters. And God said, let there be light: and there was light (Genesis 1:1-3).

2. Night and day cannot co-exist at the same time. The night must give way for the day. Your night will not be perpetual, because your day of separation from darkness and night has come (Genesis 1:4). You are a child of light—so let your light shine before others now (Matthew 5:16). Rise, declare it, and let it shine.

3. You were not born for sorrow. There is joy for you today, but your sorrow must give way in order for your joy to be manifested. Psalm 30:5,11 (NKJV) says, "His anger is but for a moment, His favor is for life; weeping may endure for a night, but joy comes in the morning . . . . You have turned for me my mourning into dancing; You have put off my sackcloth and clothed me with gladness." Also read Isaiah 61:3. God's desire for you is that He be glorified in your life. How long will you remain sorrowful?

4. King Saul of Israel had to be removed for David to take the throne and reign. For that to be true, God gave David the victory in the battle with Goliath, and He rewarded David's faith by anointing him to be king. From the day that David defeated Goliath—though still a sheep keeper—his journey to kingship began, despite Saul still being the king. And despite all that Saul did against David, he could not prevent David from taking the throne (1 Chronicle 10:1-11:13). As you do God's will today, nothing shall be able to stop you. You shall be established like David, and you will surely fulfill your divine mandate with God's help.

5. When the time of your divine transformation comes, you will not be found wanting. It pleased God to take Elijah up in a whirlwind so that Elisha could serve Him (2 Kings 2:1-15). Do not be afraid—you will not die before your time. Your fear of death must be driven out so that the spirit of life can reign in you.

6. King Uzziah had to die in order for Isaiah to see the glory of God and to serve as a prophet in his time (Isaiah 6:1-6). May God open your eyes today to see the obstacles that have been pulled down so far on your way to glory.

7. John the Baptist said that he had to decrease in order for Jesus Christ to increase. There was no need for him to stay any longer after fulfilling his mandate to prepare the way for the Lord (Matthew 3:1-17). Your time for honor has come—so all obstacles must give way.

8. Evil spirits and all forms of household wickedness and manipulation have to be cast out in order for the Holy Spirit

 to be fully manifested. Old wine must give way for the new wine—because the new wine is acceptable for the new vessel. You are now a new creature—desire the new wine of heaven (Matthew 9:14-17). It is the new you for your new assignment.

9. Bad friends, habits, unrighteousness, and unfaithfulness must give way for good friends, habits, and spiritual fruit to come (1 Corinthians 5:6-18; 6:9-20; 2 Corinthians 6:14-18).

10. Frivolous relationships must be rejected in order for lasting and meaningful relationships to be formed (Matthew 4:18-22; 8:18-22; 9:9). Daniel, Shadrach, Meshack and Abednego had to separate themselves from the Babylonian customs in order to receive revelations from God (Daniel 1:8-15). With immoral friends around you, it is extremely difficult to make righteous ones. Undoubtedly, your breakthrough will be delayed.

11. The food and meat of the king had to be rejected by Daniel in order for him to receive revelations from God (Daniel 1:8-9).

12. The spirit of mistakes, errors, and failure must give way for the spirit of success and progress to rule. The spirit of refusal, denial, and abandonment must give way for the spirit of acceptance to reign. When we confess our sins and forsake them, God immediately acts by accepting us as His children and gives us the rights of heirs. God's acceptance must rule in us, and must be seen in us.

13. The spirit of destruction must give way to the spirit of building up (Job 22:29).

14. The spirit of curse—which is the spirit of stubbornness and rejection of Jesus Christ as Lord—must give way for the spirit of blessing (Deuteronomy 28:1-15).

15. The lion had to die in order for Samson to have honey to eat and weapons to fight with.

16. The Red Sea had to part in order for the children of Israel to pass through on dry ground on their way to the Promised Land.

17. The wall of Jericho had to fall in order for the children of Israel to enter the Promised Land and possess their inheritance.

18. The spirit of bitterness must give way for the spirit of love (2 Kings 2:19-22). Total forgiveness must wipe away all forms of bitterness.

19. King Herod had to die so that Christ Jesus and His earthly parents could return to Nazareth (Matthew 2:19-23). The adversary that prevents you from doing God's will must be prayed out of your way.

20. King Herod Agrippa had to die in order for the apostles to spread the Word of God in Jerusalem (Acts 12:20-24). God will receive glory as you set out today to serve Him with all the good deeds He gives you to do. He will open the ways for you.

21. Though the men in the boat with Jonah tried to save themselves, they could not until Jonah was thrown off of the ship (Jonah 1:11-15). How many efforts are you putting into

 solving that certain problem that confounds you? Have you considered the Jonah inside? Throw him into the sea and you will have an immediate calm.

22. Jonah had to humble himself before God and pray before the fish could vomit him out (Jonah 2:10). You must also humbly pray to God, and He will deliver you from the Devil's grasp.

23. In Genesis 21:10, Sarah said, "Cast out this bondwoman and her son: for the son of this bondwoman shall not be heir with my son, even with Isaac." Abraham was reluctant in accepting that, but it was necessary in order to bring peace to his house, safety to his family, and security to Isaac's birthright.

24. The Holy Spirit had to come upon the apostles in order for their timidity, fear, and uncertainty to go away (Acts 2:1-4). Come, O Holy Ghost, and drive out fearfulness as well!

25. King Solomon in Proverbs 28:28 says, "When the wicked rise, men hide themselves: but when they perish, the righteous increase." The wicked had to be prayed out for the righteous to increase.

26. When the Holy Ghost came upon the apostles, they began to speak in new tongues, cultural barriers were broken, communication problems were overcome, and they were emboldened to declare the Word of God. The church began to form, the people were healed and delivered from sin, and the gospel spread (Acts 2-3).

In Matthew 7:5 (NKJV) Jesus taught, "First remove the plank from your own eye, and then you will see clearly to remove the speck from your brother's eye." Identify those things that have to give way in your life, and deal with them. A proper identification of your problem will lead you to a more swift and effective resolution.

The things that can be shaken within you must be removed. Every unpleasant thing must give way to the things that inspire the joy and praise of our Lord Jesus Christ.

> You have not come to the mountain that may be touched and that burned with fire, and to blackness and darkness and tempest . . . But you have come to Mount Zion and to the city of the living God, the heavenly Jerusalem, to an innumerable company of angels, to the general assembly and church of the firstborn who are registered in heaven, to God the Judge of all, to the spirits of just men made perfect, to Jesus the Mediator of the new covenant, and to the blood of sprinkling that speaks better things than that of Abel (Hebrews 12:18,22-24 NKJV).

God has given you the power to cast out all forms of evil, and you must surely do so as swiftly as possible. Jesus warns, "Every plant which My heavenly Father has not planted will be uprooted" (Matthew 15:13 NKJV). Identify the evil plants in your home, family, life, or business—and speak the Word of God against them.

We learn in Luke 10:19 (NKJV), "Behold, I give you the authority to trample on serpents and scorpions, and over all the power of the enemy, and nothing shall by any means hurt you." Victory is sure for you. The innumerable angels of God are there to back you up. The church is also there to support you. God—the Judge of all—is ready to review your case and rule in your favor. The Spirit of justice is ready to justify you. And Jesus Christ is at your side with the new covenant He has promised you. He has abolished the old covenant and His blood testifies to your inheritance in Him.

All things are possible to the person who believes. In the kingdom of God, nothing works without a living and active faith. This is because nothing can stand before a man or a woman who truly trusts in God. Faith conquers, strengthens, empowers, and emboldens the heart, and it is able to deliver believers from the trials of the Enemy. Faith frees the heart from defeat and fear. Faith can survive the fiery darts of enemies, can defeat sin, and can dispel doubts. Faith is indispensable for believers who desire to pursue God's will for their life.

Fight in faith, pray in faith, fast in faith, and live in faith. And trust in the Word of God, "For the word of God is living and powerful, and sharper than any two-edged sword, piercing even to the division of soul and spirit, and of joints and marrow, and is a discerner of the thoughts and intents of the heart" (Hebrews 4:12 NKJV).

Spend time in the presence of God until He shows you, through the Holy Spirit, the spiritual or physical obstacle that is impeding your progress. You should be ready to do away with whatever it is immediately so that God can perfect your ways. He will also reveal the Devil's strongholds in your life, and will show you the way to freedom.

Every house, every street, every county, and every nation will remain sinful and lost without Christ unless someone rises to stand against evil. The time is short, and you cannot afford to remain the same.

Chapter 8
Thirty-six Tactics Used by the Devil

I heard many mocking: "Fear on every side!" "Report," they say, "and we will report it!" All my acquaintances watched for my stumbling, saying, "Perhaps he can be induced; then we will prevail against him, and we will take our revenge on him." But the Lord is with me as a mighty, awesome One. Therefore my persecutors will stumble, and will not prevail. They will be greatly ashamed, for they will not prosper. Their everlasting confusion will never be forgotten (Jeremiah 20:10-11 NKJV.)

The Devil knows who he is—though he would never dare disclose his true identity to anyone. He always hides under a smokescreen in order to afflict his victims—the beloved brethren of Christ Jesus. Thank God that the Bible exposes him and his tactics to the church.

The devices of the Devil are multiple and complex in nature. They have the sole aim of making the children of God useless to the kingdom of God—so soiled by sinfulness, depressed by selfishness, or cynical from suffering that no one would take heed of our testimony.

Revelation 12:12 (NKJV) tells us, "Rejoice, O heavens, and you who dwell in them! Woe to the inhabitants of the earth and the sea! For the devil has come down to you, having great wrath, because he knows that he has a short time."

CHAPTER 8

There was great joy in heaven the day that the Devil was defeated and thrown out after his revolt against God. Joy and peace reign in heaven, while there is woe for the inhabitants of earth to this day. Yet, through the help of God, we must also take a decisive action against the Devil if we wish to experience peace and joy.

The Devil is unrepentant in all his ways. Unless he is dealt with decisively, he will not leave you alone. Thus God sent Christ Jesus, that we, through faith in Him, can also defeat the Devil every day of our life.

Remember that Jesus Christ does not have to fight the Devil again. He has— once and for all—fought him, defeated him, and claimed the triumph of salvation on our behalf (Isaiah 53). However, we fight him daily through our belief, our prayers in Jesus' name, and our faith in the victory on the cross.

We will overcome, but only through Christ Jesus, and with His help. The angels testified of defeating the Enemy by the blood of the Lamb and by the word of their testimonies. We can defeat him as well—any time, any day, and in any situation he might use to discourage or defeat us—because we have heavenly assistance to overcome him.

We find from Revelation 12:7-9 (NKJV),

> War broke out in heaven: Michael and his angels fought with the dragon; and the dragon and his angels fought, but they did not prevail, nor was a place found for them in heaven any longer. So the great dragon was cast out, that serpent of old, called the Devil and Satan, who deceives the whole world; he was cast to the earth, and his angels were cast out with him.

The result of the battle was sweet. [1] The Devil was defeated. [2] The Devil did not prevail against the angels of

God. [3] The army of the Enemy was cast out of heaven and will be completely destroyed. [4] The Devil has no place to return to in heaven and will be completely destroyed as well.

I pray you will overcome him as well. There are good physical and spiritual rewards for those who will overcome him.

Thirty-six tactics the Devil uses against believers

Although the Devil is as dangerous as a roaring lion, his first approach is usually as subtle and harmless as a dove. In the book of Revelation, we are instructed that we must overcome the Devil whether he comes as a beast to devour us, an image to mesmerize us, or a mark to own us. No matter what his underhanded ways, we have to identify them, resist them, and defeat him in Jesus' name.

1. The Devil comes like a roaring lion to devour—(through frightening experiences) either spiritually, through dreams, through physical problems, or through emotional sickness. But in all these things, we can overcome his onslaughts through Christ Jesus

2. He comes as a thief in your unguarded moment to steal and as a destroyer to demolish your life, property, and other precious possessions in your family and business. But with God, you are more than a conqueror through Christ who loves you.

3. The Enemy comes as a sweeping flood—inundating you with numerous problems at a time. But the Spirit of God shall lift up a standard against him.

 4. He may work through foolish decisions and confused words. But when we turn to God thereafter, He will defend us and the Devil will flee. In Hosea 4:6, the Lord says, "My people are destroyed for lack of knowledge." Yet, where God dwells and His knowledge reigns, the Devil is conspicuously absent.

5. Satan also attacks through multiple and false visions which might look true to an ordinary man, or the complete lack of a godly vision in any matter. Yet we know from Proverbs 29:18, "Where there is no vision, the people perish." "We see in part, and prophesy in part, but when Christ comes, we shall see clearly" (1 Corinthians 13:12). God can turn our mountains into level ground. He can fill in our valleys and make our crooked ways straight when we turn to Him in true repentance and trust.

6. He attacks us whether we are in great prosperity or in abject poverty. He has no respect for any man. However, he fears Christ Jesus, and he will flee from those that have the guts to resist him in Jesus' name (Ezekiel 16:49-50).

7. The Devil tries to deceive us when we have no counsel, and he gains a foothold when we act upon ungodly counsel. Remember that with much godly counsel there is safety (Psalm 1:1).

8. He can work through friends, your spouse, family members, business partners, and other relationships to tempt you to sin. Do not consent to their words or advice. Rather, watch and pray (Psalm 55:12-14).

9. The Enemy will entice you to false worship. He manifests himself as an angel of light in order to deceive the faithful. We should try all spirits to discern which is of God. Be very careful about who you trust (Luke 4:5-8).

10. He discourages you through tribulations, distress, persecutions, false accusations, famine, and other perils. But Jesus says, "Be of good cheer; I have overcome the world" (John 16:33).

11. The Devil sneaks in through the unguarded windows of your life. Thank God for giving you the authority to expel him through Christ Jesus. Pray and guard against all forms of unwanted spiritual intruders (Matthew 16:22-23).

12. He thwarts your progress by interrupting your prayer life and your time for Bible study. He introduces seemingly good alternatives—business opportunities, sports, entertainment, recreation, profit-making ventures, and so on. The Devil knows how to keep a person busy through many unprofitable spiritual and physical activities. Therefore, make your prayer and Bible study time a priority every day. This is the only way to have sound spiritual guidance (1 Corinthians 10:1-12).

13. Satan works against your faith by prearranging negative results and creating discouragements. Be focused, be determined, and be very courageous. Your day of joy is coming very soon (1 Kings 18:41-45).

14. He frustrates your Christian walk through delays in your plans, visions, and dreams. He has used this method quite often; however, it usually backfires on him. Most of his

 victims end up with a greater victory through faith in Christ and determination. Therefore, hold on to Christ Jesus—He alone can make a way in the wilderness for you and bring you to the Promised Land of triumph.

15. The Devil tries to hinder you through falsehoods and unholy alternatives. Know that the Devil is the father of lies. Yet, Jesus Christ is the Truth. Hold on to the truth of Christ Jesus, and He will speak on your behalf (Luke 4:2-4).

16. He tries to hurt you through sickness, oppression, denial, sorrow, weakness, condemnation, and even death. But rejoice, for Jesus Christ is the Lord of lords in all situations (John 10:10).

17. The Enemy attempts to seize you through rejections, unholy associations, blood covenants, and initiations. But the blood of Jesus separates you from wickedness completely, and He gives you a new life of righteousness and freedom (Daniel 1:1-9).

18. He confuses you through children, house helpers, gossips, unhealthy habits, unseemly ideas, and so on. But give thanks to God who gives you victory against all of the darts of the Devil.

19. He tempts you to compromise your Christian ethics—keeping that little bit of hatred or malice, speaking evil against another, or secretly lusting in your heart (Jeremiah 35:1-10).

20. To Adam and Eve in the garden, he came questioning God's commands as a test to their obedience to God (Genesis 3:1-5).

21. To Adam and Eve, Satan came as a companion and an advisor. They were unable to resist him, but God has a provided for our victory in Christ Jesus (Genesis 3:1-5).

22. To Sarah and Hannah, the Devil came in the form of a temporary barrenness. The same God who miraculously opened their wombs and gave them children is the One we serve today.

23. To the daughters of Lot, he deceived them into believing that there were no men to marry. Because of that, they tricked their father and sinned with him (Genesis 19:30-38).

24. The Enemy tried to discourage Ruth through her early widowhood. But God turned it into a blessing for the whole world. She gave birth to Obed, who was the father of Jesse, who was the father of David—all of which were in the family lineage of Jesus Christ (Ruth 1:15-22).

25. To Samson, the enticement came in the form of a beautiful woman when he was in dire need of love. To you, it may be the need of a wife or a husband (Judges 16).

26. To Noah, the temptation came in the form of sweet wine after his great victory of surviving the flood. How many today fall to alcohol or drugs under the guise of celebration or of entertaining friends and business partners (Genesis 9:20-21)?

27. For David, the Enemy took advantage of a time of leisure after attaining greatness as the king of Israel (2 Samuel 11:1-27; 13:1-36)

 28. To Absalom, the lure was the popularity and power that he could receive from being the king. He did not mind the cost for achieving his selfish desires—even if it meant disgracing and sacrificing his father, David. Today, people still abandon their family members for money and fame (2 Samuel 15:1-23).

29. He discouraged and enslaved the Israelites through a severe famine. They were in bondage, maltreated, and slaughtered by the Egyptians (Genesis 46:1-27).

30. And he cause the great suffering of Job through the destruction of all his cattle, the collapse of his business, the death of all his children, the rejection from his wife, and the pain and sickness that ate away at his bones. Thank God, he remained firm in his faith and earned a greater reward at the end (Job 1:13-20).

31. He tormented Shadrach, Meshach, Abednego, and Daniel with false accusations. He tried to prevent them from praying to almighty God; tried to annihilate Shadrach, Meshach, and Abednego in the burning fiery furnace; and tried to destroy Daniel in the lion's den. Thank God for delivering them, and that their testimonies are still available to encourage us today (Daniel 3:8-25; 6:11-24).

32. To Judas Iscariot, the inducement came in the form of wealth. Judas did not realize the true cost of his lies (Matthew 26:14-16).

33. He tried to thwart Peter by filling him with fear to the point that the apostle denied Christ three times the night Jesus was tried and sent to the cross (Matthew 26:69-75).

34. To dissuade the other disciples of Jesus Christ, the Enemy incited the serious persecution of the church by the rulers and religious zealots of that time. However, as the Lord Jesus has promised, "The gates of Hades shall not prevail against it" (Matthew 16:18 NKJV; also see Acts 5:40; 9:1-3; 16:22-24).

35. And Satan went to Jesus Christ while He was in the wilderness—to tempt Him through His intense hunger and weakness after forty days of fasting. The Tempter also pretended to be an admirer in order to entice Jesus and sway Him from His path to the cross. Yet, Satan failed—thanks be to God (Luke 4:1-13)!

36. The Enemy may come in a unique way to you, but stand firm! Victory is yours (John 8:44)!

Check your anger, confusion, quarrelsome attitude, hatred, loneliness, joblessness, sadness, urges, entertainment, lack, and bad feelings. The Devil may be trying to get at you through them. Yet you are given godly advice in 1 Peter 5:6-9 (NKJV),

Therefore humble yourselves under the mighty hand of God, that He may exalt you in due time, casting all your care upon Him, for He cares for you. Be sober; be vigilant; because your adversary the devil walks about like a roaring lion, seeking whom he may devour. Resist him, steadfast in the faith, knowing that the same sufferings are experienced by your brotherhood in the world.

 Ephesians 6:13-18 (NIV) gives us all the weapons we need for an absolute victory in all satanic battles.

> **Therefore put on the full armor of God, so that when the day of evil comes, you may be able to stand your ground, and after you have done everything, to stand. Stand firm then, with the belt of truth buckled around your waist, with the breastplate of righteousness in place, and with your feet fitted with the readiness that comes from the gospel of peace. In addition to all this, take up the shield of faith, with which you can extinguish all the flaming arrows of the evil one. Take the helmet of salvation and the sword of the Spirit, which is the word of God. And pray in the Spirit on all occasions with all kinds of prayers and requests. With this in mind, be alert and always keep on praying for all the saints.**

Chapter 9
The Road to Calvary's Cross

One day in a revelation, I was taken to a place that was infinitely more glorious and beautiful than this present world. I presume it was heaven. The road to the place was very narrow, and along the roadside were many dangerous animals that I was afraid of.

I asked my guide why the animals were there, and I was told to take my eyes off the animals and to keep following the guide. That the animals had no power to harm anyone who kept moving along the road. However, they could overpower a person who stopped.

On the way to heaven, you are to keep moving until you get there—no retreating or sidetracking is permitted. And you are always to keep your eyes on the Lord Jesus Christ. He is your only true guide—the Author and Finisher of your faith—who said, "As the Father knoweth me, even so know I the Father: and I lay down my life for the sheep" (John 10:15). And we are admonished,

Since we are surrounded by so great a cloud of witnesses, let us lay aside every weight, and the sin which so easily ensnares us, and let us run with endurance the race that is set before us, looking unto Jesus, the author and finisher of our faith, who for the joy that was set before Him endured the cross, despising the shame, and has sat down at the right hand of the throne of God. For consider Him who endured such hostility from sinners against Himself, lest you become weary and discouraged in your souls (Hebrews 12:1-3 NKJV).

At Calvary, Jesus Christ paid the ultimate price—death on a cross—to save whoever would believe in Him and put their trust in Him alone. The price to redeem humanity—to make us free and acceptable before God in heaven—was His blood. "The law requires that nearly everything be cleansed with blood, and without the shedding of blood there is no forgiveness" (Hebrews 9:22 NIV).

He paid the price in order to confirm His absolute love for us. And no other sacrifice was acceptable to God—only that which Christ Jesus offered. In Acts 4:12(NKJV), Peter said, "There is no other name under heaven given among men by which we must be saved." In Acts 5:30-31 (NKJV), he also said, "The God of our fathers raised up Jesus whom you murdered by hanging on a tree. Him God has exalted to His right hand to be Prince and Savior, to give repentance to Israel and forgiveness of sins."

In accepting to bear our guilt upon Himself, He bought us freedom, salvation, deliverance from sin, victory over the Devil, breakthrough, prosperity, health, peace, and progress. "Christ was offered once to bear the sins of many. To those who eagerly wait for Him He will appear a second time, apart from sin, for salvation" (Hebrews 9:28).

His journey to the cross actually began at the synagogue in Nazareth, on the Sabbath when He declared the following purpose for His coming to the earth.

The Spirit of the Lord is upon Me, because He has anointed Me to preach the gospel to the poor; He has sent

Me to heal the brokenhearted, to proclaim liberty to the captives and recovery of sight to the blind, to set at liberty those who are oppressed; to proclaim the acceptable year of the Lord (Luke 4:18-20 NKJV).

If you are outside of Christ Jesus, the Devil does not worry about you, because you are already his prey. All those who choose to remain outside of the will of God belong to the Devil and will surely do his bidding.

However, the moment you declare your trust in Jesus Christ, the Devil sets his eyes upon you for destruction. His goal is to annihilate anything or anyone who belongs to God. In fact, the Devil followed Jesus all the way to the prayer garden of Gethsemane and finally to the place of skull called Golgotha—where Jesus was crucified. Satan thought he had triumphed there—he thought that he had succeeded in destroying the Son of God. Yet, he was very, very wrong—and the resurrection proved it. Thank God for your victory through Jesus Christ.

Things That Befell Our Lord Jesus Christ

1. The weight of our sin was so heavy upon Him that He was overwhelmed with sorrow. He went to the Father in prayer three times, and asked for the cup of death to be taken away from Him. Yet, each time He prayed for the Father's will to be done and accepted the path to the cross (Matthew 26:36-50).

2. His companion and disciple, Judas Iscariot, betrayed him—yet He betrayed no one (Matthew 26:48).

3. His captors laid their hands upon Him for no reason (Matthew 26:50).

4. He was arrested like a criminal for a crime He never committed.

5. His disciples forsook Him, and He was required to bear His cross and punishment alone (Matthew 26:56).

6. Unfounded accusations were used against Him, and ended in His complete condemnation. Though all the allegations were false, He did not dispute any of them (Matthew 26:59).

7. The King of all kings and the Lord above all other lords, was judged by the carnal spiritual heads of Israel and by Pilate so that we would not be judged (Matthew 26:62).

8. Jesus was condemned by the spiritual leaders of those days for daring to declare His mission on earth. Matthew 26:66 testifies, "They answered and said, He is guilty of death." Matthew 27:22 also shows, "They all say unto him, Let him be crucified." And Jesus accepted their guilty verdict so that we would be made free from all forms of condemnation.

9. The soldiers and the people spat in His face—humiliating and disgracing Him (Matthew 26:67).

10. He was treated badly—the people buffeted and beat Him with the palms of their hands and their fists (Matthew 26:67).

11. Despite the fact that He had already been arrested and was being kept in custody, the chief priests and the elders still took evil counsel against Him (Matthew 27:1).

12. His freedom was completely denied, and He was delivered to Pontius Pilate for final judgment (Matthew 27:2).

13. He was imprisoned on our behalf (Matthew 27:15-26).

14. He was thoroughly scourged (Matthew 27:26).

15. He was stripped naked and humiliated. He took on the humiliation that we should have experienced because of our sin (Matthew 27:28).

16. A crown of thorns was forced upon His head—mocking his Kingship and Lordship. They pierced Him and He bled (Matthew 27:29-30).

17. He carried the cross He was crucified on (Matthew 27:32).

18. The cruelest form of torture and punishment—He was nailed upon the cross and was left suspended upon it until He died (Matthew 27:33-50).

19. They gave Him sour vinegar wine mixed with gall to drink twice (Matthew 27:34,48).

20. Even when He was on the cross, men still mocked Him (Matthew 27:36-44).

21. He cried aloud twice while on the cross (Matthew 27:46,50).

22. To confirm His death, His side was pierced with a spear (John 19:34).

 He accepted all of these things—not because He was guilty, but because we were all guilty, and He had to pay the price for our guilt. He endured it all in order to set us free. John 8:36 (NKJV) assures, "If the Son makes you free, you shall be free indeed."

Jesus Christ once met a woman condemned to death for adultery. His verdict to her is the same He gives to us, "Neither do I condemn thee: go, and sin no more" (John 8:11).

The Devil has made this world a wilderness—he decimates and enslaves cities and families. He holds them captive, and refuses to open the door of escape (Isaiah 14:17).

But thanks to God the Father for giving us Jesus Christ who is always able and willing to set us free. "The key of the house of David I will lay on his shoulder; so he shall open, and no one shall shut; and he shall shut, and no one shall open" (Isaiah 22:22 NKJV).

The reason for Jesus' torture and subsequent death on the cross of Calvary was that we might be saved from the hands of the Devil and from all of our adversaries. "For God so love the world, that he gave his only begotten Son, that whosoever believeth in him should not perish, but have everlasting life. For God sent not his Son into the world to condemn the world; but that the world through him might be saved" (John 3:16-17).

Therefore, accept Jesus Christ now!

Chapter 10
The Place of Prayer

Prayer builds a Christian's confidence and gives him or her the endurance to face the onslaught of the Enemy until victory comes. Of course, the works of the adversary shall not continue forever—they will be brought down and ended by your prayers. However, don't expect any relief until you pray. Your wishes may be good but they are not prayers. Open your heart and mouth to God in sincere and open conversation. Communicate constantly with God in private and out in the open through prayers.

At one time, when king Ahab was on the throne of Israel, Elijah prayed for the rain to cease. First Kings 17 confirms that God answered Elijah's prayer, and that it did not rain In Israel for three and a half years.

However, when the same Elijah wanted rain, he had to pray it down. First Kings 18:41 (NKJV) tells us, "Elijah said to Ahab, 'Go up, eat and drink; for there is the sound of abundance of rain.'" The king heard no sound of rain, and there was no physical sign of any, but the prophet of God had given his word. Yet, for his words to be true, Elijah had to pray.

So he went to a place where there was no interruption or distraction. "Elijah went up to the top of Carmel; and he cast himself down upon the earth, and put his face between his knees" (1 Kings 18:41 NKJV). Elijah put his face between his knees so he could avoid being discouraged. He communicated with God in faith, and did not allow his eyes or ears to divert his attention. And he prayed.

His servant—acting on Elijah's instructions—came back six times to report whether he had seen any sign of rain—even a cloud. He had not. But Elijah was adamant, and he told the servant to go back and observe the horizon a seventh time.

It was then that the word came. "There is a cloud, as small as a man's hand, rising out of the sea!" (1 Kings 18:44 NKJV).

Don't ever stop praying until the answer comes. Always pray until something happens.

The Lord gave me a revelation to take His gospel to the nations of the world, but I prayed for nine years before the doors were opened to me to carry out His instructions. Those nine years were filled with all sorts of difficulties, trials, confusion, tears, and a tremendous waste of resources. But the hope and the belief that His words would come to pass kept me praying and fasting. And now I can testify to others and write this book with some of the experiences I gained during this time. The same God that answered Elijah's prayers and my prayers will answer yours as well.

Satanic conflicts against God's faithful ones date back to when Satan was expelled from heaven—driven from the very presence of God. His onslaught against Adam and Eve in the Garden of Eden brought sin into the world. This resulted in the degeneration and death of mankind, and the subsequent separation of people from God. The fall also brought us hardship, toilsome labor, lack, inferiority, and it completely took away the peace that Adam had with God in the garden.

The victory of our Lord Jesus Christ against the Devil brought us back into a right relationship with God—as we were before sin entered the world. It brought back peace and joy, and gave us hope for eternity.

Adam fell because he disobeyed God's commands. Jesus Christ succeeded because He obeyed the will of God. He is the true manifestation of the Word of God—and He is God, Himself.

Death came into the world through the sin of Adam. Life came back into the world through the obedience of Jesus Christ.

Through the fall of Adam, condemnation, sorrow, and pain took hold of mankind. Through the resurrection of Jesus Christ, acceptance, peace, and joy are restored unto humanity.

Paul, in Romans 5:12,14,17-19 (NKJV) says,

> Therefore, just as through one man sin entered the world, and death through sin, and thus death spread to all men, because all sinned . . . Nevertheless death reigned from Adam to Moses, even over those who had not sinned according to the likeness of the transgression of Adam, who is a type of Him who was to come. . . . For if by the one man's offense death reigned through the one, much more those who receive abundance of grace and of the gift of righteousness will reign in life through the One, Jesus Christ. Therefore, as through one man's offense judgment came to all men, resulting in condemnation, even so through one Man's righteous act the free gift came to all men, resulting in justification of life. For as by one man's disobedience many were made sinners, so also by one Man's obedience many will be made righteous.

CHAPTER 10

Prayer is very important to us as Christians—particularly if we want to make any meaningful progress in this life. The result of prayer is to quicken us to God's ways. However, we must also obey His Word. As Samuel told King Saul, "To obey is better than sacrifice" (1 Samuel 15:22).

The ancients engaged their enemies in physical combat. However, when Christ came, He engaged the Devil through prayers and fasting—giving us a new example to follow. Jesus Christ never took up arms against anyone.

When the guards came to arrest Jesus in the garden of Gethsemane, Peter wanted to defend Him. Yet, He advised Peter to put down his sword. He told Peter to rely upon the help that is from God, which is far more powerful than any earthly means. And though the Enemy appeared to have won, the illusion was very brief. God had the ultimate victory when He raised Jesus from the grave just three days later. Your triumph will not be any different.

Jesus Christ once told His disciples that there are some demons that can never be cast out, except through prayer and fasting (Matthew 17:21). Jesus Christ, on several occasions, combined fasting with praying—and the apostles followed His example. He told the disciples that faith in God and prayers can uproot all mountains. However, prayer requires faith, righteousness, continuity, perseverance, and your obedience to God in order to produce results.

Through intimacy and continuous fellowship, the disciples of Jesus Christ observed and imitated His prayer life. They also asked Him to teach them how to pray (Luke 11:1).

Brethren, there is power in prayer that produces great results and moves mountains. The length of your prayers is immaterial. Rather, it is the condition of your heart and the strength of your faith that matter most. Prayer that flows from a pure heart is acceptable to God and will surely produce results.

Since we are encouraged to emulate Christ Jesus in all things, we also should use prayer as an effective weapon of spiritual warfare. Paul said, "We do not wrestle against flesh and blood, but against principalities, against powers, against the rulers of the darkness of this age, against spiritual hosts of wickedness in the heavenly places" (Ephesians 6:12 NKJV).

We know that the weapon of prayer is particularly effective for standing against the principalities and powers of spiritual darkness and for making us victorious over them. "The weapons of our warfare are not carnal, but mighty through God to the pulling down of strong holds; casting down imaginations, and every high thing that exalteth itself against the knowledge of God, and bringing into captivity every thought to the obedience of Christ" (2 Corinthians 10:4-5).

Jesus Christ, our Lord, used prayer to achieve all that He accomplished for mankind. He purposefully came in the flesh to show that we can do as He did—we can overcome the Devil through prayer and faith. He came to show us the way. "Most assuredly, I say to you, he who believes in Me, the works that I do he will do also; and greater works than these he will do, because I go to My Father" (John 14:12 NKJV).

The apostles established their callings through prayer, and saw great wonders in their respective ministries. The prophets of God saw great miracles through their prayers. So they continued in them and communicated their importance to subsequent generations. The testimonies generated by heartfelt, obedient prayer abound in others, and can abound in you as well—if only you will pray. You too can testify to the power of prayer.

Prayer occurs when you address your words to God through Jesus Christ. In order to honor God, you should give your absolute attention and full concentration to Him while you are praying.

Jesus Christ was always praying, but sometimes He had to separate Himself from the people in order to give His full attention to the Father (Luke 6:12; 9:28). "When he had sent them away, he departed into a mountain to pray" (Mark 6:46).

Jesus Christ advised the disciples not to give up praying, but, "Ask, and it shall be given you; seek, and ye shall find; knock, and it shall be opened unto you" (Matthew 7:7). He said that if they kept asking—their requests would be granted. If they kept knocking—all closed doors would be opened to them. And if they kept seeking—they would surely find everything they were looking for. They just needed to continue on in prayer until their answers were received.

Jesus also taught:

- "Whatever things you ask in prayer, believing, you will receive" (Matthew 21:22 NKJV).

- "If two of you agree on earth concerning anything that they ask, it will be done for them by My Father in heaven" (Matthew 18:19 NKJV).

- "Whatever things you ask when you pray, believe that you receive them, and you will have them" (Mark 11:24 NKJV).

Many of us are waiting for signs to confirm that God has

answered us before we completely believe that He has. This is wrong. Jesus said that when you pray, you must believe that God has answered. Faith in His promise to answer you is all you need—not signs. Signs will come latter.

The Bible encourages us to pray continuously, to give ourselves to uninterrupted daily prayer, and to pray in all things. There is nothing too small to pray about or to trust God for—and there is nothing too big that prayer cannot handle.

- "Evening, and morning, and at noon, will I pray, and cry aloud: and he shall hear my voice" (Psalm 55:17).

- "O you who hear prayer, to you all men will come" (Psalm 65:2 NIV).

- "We will give ourselves continually to prayer, and to the ministry of the word" (Acts 6:4).

- "Peter was therefore kept in prison, but constant prayer was offered to God for him by the church" (Acts 12:5 NKJV).

- "Praying always with all prayer and supplication in the Spirit, being watchful to this end with all perseverance and supplication for all the saints" (Ephesians 6:18 NKJV).

- "I will therefore that men pray everywhere, lifting up holy hands, without wrath and doubting" (1 Timothy 2:8).

Don't ever stop praying. And don't worry about the circumstances surrounding you—they cannot stop God from answering. The moment you give up, or are discouraged about praying, you run the risk of giving in to defeat

 (Luke 18:1; Philippians 4:6; James 5:13,16).

Brethren, your previously disappointing experiences in prayer do not matter—neither does what other people might say or think. God still answers prayers—and He will certainly answer you.

"When I shut up heaven and there be no rain, or command the locusts to devour the land, or send pestilence among my people, If my people, who are called by my name, will humble themselves, and pray, and seek my face, and turn from their wicked ways; then I will hear from heaven, and will forgive their sin, and heal their land. Now my eyes will be open and my ears attentive to prayer made in this place" (2 Chronicles 7:13-15).

How to pray

What is prayer? Prayer is primarily communication with God about all things. It may involve asking, knocking, and seeking God's help. Jesus Christ gave us the key to receiving answers to our prayers in John 14:13-14 (NKJV), "Whatever you ask in My name, that I will do, that the Father may be glorified in the Son. If you ask anything in My name, I will do it."

He also said, "You did not choose me, but I chose you and appointed you that you should go and bear fruit, and that your fruit should remain, that whatever you ask the Father in My name He may give you" (John 15:16 NKJV).

The name of Jesus is highly exalted, and one day every knee will bow at the mention of His name—whether in heaven, or on earth, or under the earth.

Only prayer can change things permanently. Prayer brings back the glory of God and destroys the plans of the Devil (Philippians 2:8-11).

Conditions for effective prayer

1. Pray continually in and for all things (Luke 18:7-8).

2. When you pray, absolutely believe in God's ability and desire to give you an answer. Believe that your prayer has been heard and that you have received the desired result. This is what it means to act in faith. Remember, prayer does not cause faith to work; rather, faith causes prayer to work. Pray right.

3. Forgive others without attaching any conditions. Do not hold any grudges against anyone. This allows the Spirit of God to have freedom to work in you and to prevent the Devil from gaining a stronghold. This also clears the way for all of your prayers to be answered (Mark 11:25).

4. Pray in the Spirit and in your understanding (Romans 8:25; 1 Corinthians 14:15; Ephesians 6:18).

Prayer is actually petition, thanksgiving, and praises unto God. The book of Psalms reveals David's prayer life—how he struggled with God, but also how he adored his Lord.

Your world will only collapse if your knees refuse to bend for prayer. When prayer ceases, unseen evil takes over. Thus the wisdom of 1 Thessalonians 5:17-19 (NKJV), "Pray without ceasing, in everything give thanks; for this is the will of God in Christ Jesus for you. Do not quench the Spirit."

Four essentials of prayer

1. The presence of the Holy Spirit. Praying in the Spirit means praying according to the will of God. The Spirit discloses the heart of God and directs us to pray aright. He

 helps us to continue praying until we receive an answer to our petitions. Where the Spirit dwells, God also dwells—because the Spirit is God. However, He can only dwell in a pure and clean heart. Romans 8:26 (NKJV) says, "Likewise the spirit also helps in our weaknesses. For we do not know what we should pray for as we ought, but the Spirit Himself makes intercession for us with groanings which cannot be uttered." That is why God gives us the Spirit at repentance and baptism. Peter said in Acts 2:38 "Repent, and be baptized every one of you in the name of Jesus Christ for the remission of sins, and ye shall receive the gift of the Holy Ghost."

2. A right heart. When the heart is not right, the prayer will be wrong as well. A right heart is one where Jesus Christ dwells and reigns. It is a born again heart—a renewed heart. It is a heart that seeks God first before any other. It is not fixed on evil or the reward of evil; rather, it is fixed on Jesus, and He directs it through the Spirit. Solomon said in Proverbs 20:27 (NKJV), "The spirit of man is the lamp of the Lord, searching all the inner depths of the heart."

3. The Word of God. The proper understanding and application of the Word of God in prayer guarantees an answer. The Word is powerful and unfailing. It accomplishes all that it is sent to do. The Word is God, Himself (John 1:1). When you have a problem, locate its source, find the Scripture that best fits it, apply the Scripture to your problem, and it will be solved. The Word of God solves all the problems of humanity. It settles all things and gives light and understanding to every issue. As we learn in Matthew 24:35, it is eternal. "Heaven and earth shall pass away, but my words shall not pass away."

4. You don't know how important you are to God until you are born again and start participating actively in prayer. You will not grasp the full effect of your prayers until you begin to communicate with God with all of your heart. Luke18:1 tells us, "Men ought always to pray." Matthew 6:6 (NIV) teaches, "When you pray, go into your room, close the door and pray to your Father, who is unseen. Then your Father, who sees what is done in secret, will reward you." It is essential that you recognize Jesus Christ as your only Lord and Savior, and often bow your knees to Him in prayer. You best understand your heart's desires, and God wants to listen to you—however, you must pray.

Wishes don't solve problems, but prayer does. When you actively participate in solving your problems through prayer, you will know how to keep such problems from coming back. However, when you don't actively participate in solving your problems, you will have only occasional or temporary victories. Let your solutions be permanent, pray them out for yourself—and obey every aspect of God's instructions concerning them.

As we know from Romans 10:8-9 (NIV), "'The word is near you; it is in your mouth and in your heart,' that is, the word of faith we are proclaiming: That if you confess with your mouth, 'Jesus is Lord,' and believe in your heart that God raised him from the dead, you will be saved."

The essence of this book is to help you reach your God-given victory through knowledge and prayer. Rise up and pray in Jesus' name, for your day of victory has come.

Some results of prayer

Earlier in this book, we studied the fact that prayer

 changes all things. Let us now look at some of the things that prayer has changed.

Christ Jesus went out to pray with three of His disciples—Peter, John, and James. The Bible says that while the disciples slept, Jesus prayed and was changed physically by His prayers.

As he prayed, the fashion of his countenance was altered, and his raiment was white and glistering. And, behold, there talked with him two men, which were Moses and Elias: who appeared in glory, and spake of his decease which he should accomplish at Jerusalem. But Peter and they that were with him were heavy with sleep: and when they were awake, they saw his glory, and the two men that stood with him (Luke 9:29-32).

Jeremiah had great conflicts with some of the people of Jerusalem, and he almost gave up on the assignment that God had given him. But through prayer, Jeremiah regained his confidence, and had victory in his assignments. The following are his prayers and expectations.

O Lord, you deceived me, and I was deceived; you overpowered me and prevailed. I am ridiculed all day long; everyone mocks me. Whenever I speak, I cry out proclaiming violence and destruction. So the word of the Lord has brought me insult and reproach all day long. But if I say, "I will not mention him or speak any more in his name," his word is in my heart like a fire, a fire shut up in my bones. I am weary of holding it in; indeed, I cannot. I hear many whispering, "Terror on every side! Report him! Let's report him!" All my friends are waiting for me to slip, saying, "Perhaps he will be deceived; then we will prevail over him and take our revenge on him." But the Lord is with me like a mighty warrior; so my persecutors will stumble and not prevail. They will fail and be thoroughly disgraced; their dishonor will never be forgotten. O Lord Almighty, you who examine the righteous and probe the heart and mind, let me see your vengeance upon them, for to you I have committed my cause (Jeremiah 20:7-12 NIV).

The early church in Acts prevailed greatly through prayer, and had astounding results.

When they had prayed, the place was shaken where they were assembled together; and they were all filled with the Holy Ghost, and they spake the word of God with boldness . . .. And with great power gave the apostles witness of the resurrection of the Lord Jesus: and great grace was upon them all (Acts 4:31,33).

Through angelic intervention, prayer broke down that prison walls that held the apostles. "The angel of the Lord by night opened the prison doors, and brought them forth, and said, Go, stand and speak in the temple to the people all the words of this life" (Acts 5:19-20).

The same was true for Paul and Silas in Acts 16:25-26,

At midnight Paul and Silas prayed, and sang praises unto God: and the prisoners heard them. And suddenly there was a great earthquake, so that the foundations of the prison were shaken: and immediately all the doors were opened, and every one's bands were loosed.

As you pray, believe and expect that great and mighty things will occur. Miracles, deliverance, promotions, peace, and victory are all results of prayers. And they can happen for you.

I have witnessed the mighty power of God in various ways in my more than 15 years of preaching and teaching His Word. The testimony of Daniel in the lion's den—and those of Shadrach, Meshach, and Abednego, in the burning fiery furnace—are the result of steadfastness in prayer, and the determination to continually trust and honor the Lord Almighty.

A Call to Prayer

Thank God for His grace in reading this book. Now prepare yourself for prayer. Proverbs 20:18,22 (NKJV) declares, "Plans are established by counsel, by wise counsel wage war. . . . Do not say, 'I will recompense evil'; wait for the Lord, and He will save you."

This beautiful promise from the throne of grace should wake us up to desire greater things as promised by God.

Isaiah 62:1 (NKJV) says, "For Zion's sake I will not hold My peace, and for Jerusalem's sake I will not rest, until her righteousness goes forth as brightness, and her salvation as a lamp that burns."

Using the Scripture passages I have provided concerning salvation, repeat these declarations.

- I have made up my mind that from now on, I will walk with the Lord Jesus Christ.

- And I declare that I refuse to be terrified by my past and present mistakes. The Lord Jesus Christ has transformed me by washing me with His blood. All the evil in my past has gone away. I am renewed in Christ Jesus every day. My mind, spirit, thoughts, and ways have all been renewed. I am no longer on the path of destruction, sorrow, and darkness in this life. I have received the light of Jesus. And because of Him, I am a success.

▸ I refuse to be terrified by evil dreams. The Lord Jesus Christ has prepared a good path for me to walk in, and I will never walk in the path of evil again. It is well with me, in Jesus' name.

▸ I refuse to be terrified by masquerading demons and spirits. In the name of Jesus Christ, I unmask them in my business, home, life, family, and in all of my ways. I will begin to make progress in life, in Jesus' name.

▸ I refuse to be terrified by any dark family tradition practiced by my ancestors. Their actions will never affect me again from this day forward, in Jesus' name. I am a new creature—my past has been washed away and all things are now new. I begin a new and purposeful life, making progress in every area. And I will discover God's vision for my future. Today I begin to regain all of the good things that I have lost in the past, in Jesus' name.

▸ I refuse to be terrified by what I am seeing now. I am more than a conqueror through Christ Jesus. In all things, I receive victory, favor, deliverance, and a sound mind. Therefore, I will begin to make progress through the strength of Christ Jesus.

▸ I will physically, spiritually, and emotionally conquer and defeat the Devil and all of his agents against me through the blood of Jesus Christ.

▸ I demolish every satanic device against my progress in life with the blood of Jesus Christ.

▸ Through the blood of Jesus Christ, I will triumph over every satanic agent sent to drag me into failure, fear, and captivity.

▸ With the blood of Jesus Christ, I will conquer all forms of unfruitfulness in my life, marriage, business, and in the lives of all my children.

▸ I receive grace to make progress in all the things that I set my hands to do.

▸ I conquer every spirit of failure that haunts my life and my future, in Jesus' name.

▸ I conquer every unseen evil follower, in Jesus' name.

▸ I conquer every unseen evil manipulator, in Jesus' name.

▸ I am not what I use to be before, because the Lord Jesus Christ now dwells in me. He alone controls my life.

▸ I receive the spirit of adoption to cry, "Abba, Father!" and to overcome every form of spiritual fear, in Jesus' name.

▸ I conquer the spirits of shame and servitude, in Jesus' name.

▸ I refuse to be put to shame again. I reject the words of shame. I receive the spirit of boldness to stand, be counted, and be recognized. Success, progress, and godly strength will follow me from now on, in Jesus' name.

▸ In my body, I receive godly strength. In my spirit, I receive heavenly strength. In my soul, I receive refreshment from heaven.

▸ Like Daniel, who received heavenly assistance (Daniel 10:2-19), I receive heavenly assistance in everything that I do today, in Jesus' name.

▸ I receive strength, in Jesus' name; courage, in Jesus' name; peace and joy, in Jesus' name; boldness, in Jesus' name; a sound mind, in Jesus' name; and understanding, in Jesus' name.

▸ I also receive all of the benefits inherent in salvation from the throne of heaven—good health, progress, victory over all evil, and great peace, in Jesus' name.

Amen.

God changes things when we pray. Prayer in itself changes nothing, but God changes all things when we humble ourselves and look to Him in prayer. Through prayer, there are no denominational barriers, but sin stops people from depending fully on God in every thing.

Conclusion
Heaven and Hell Are Real

Run away from the strongholds of hell. Flee from all forms of sin, rage, addiction, hatred, fear, adultery, idolatry, murder, lust, fornication, false worship, deception, stubbornness, disobedience, cultism, secrecy, witchcraft, unholy associations, and all forms of evil. Decide today to close every satanic inroad into you and your concerns. This can only be done through the life you live and your daily practices.

Therefore, if you have not done so before, I invite you right now to be reconciled to the Lord Jesus Christ. He loves you, and He is calling you with open arms to embrace you. His desire is to lead you into a new life that is very productive.

James 4:7 says, "Submit yourselves therefore to God. Resist the devil, and he will flee from you."

> That if thou shalt confess with thy mouth the Lord Jesus, and shalt believe in thine heart that God hath raised him from the dead, thou shalt be saved. For with the heart man believeth unto righteousness; and with the mouth confession is made unto salvation. For the scripture saith, Whosoever believeth on him shall not be ashamed (Romans 10:9-11).

Make the right choice today. Decide to make the change that leads to everlasting life.

Everyone wants a change. Everyone can use a second

 chance. Let it begin for you right now. Renew your heart today by bringing it under the authority of the Word of God. Commit yourself to pursuing a living, active, and eternal relationship with the almighty God. Trust in Jesus Christ and read your Bible every day. Be born again, and receive the Holy Spirit.

If you would like to do so, pray this simple prayer now.

O God, today [/ / date], I accept Your offer of eternal life and a wonderful relationship with You. I confess that I have sinned and have been separated from You. I believe that Jesus Christ died on the cross for my sins and my guilt. I also believe that Jesus rose from the dead on the third day, and that You, Jesus, now sit at the right hand of the Father in heaven and intercede for me. I now turn from sins and put my trust in You for forgiveness, fulfillment, purpose and eternal life. I [name] receive You into my heart and life as my personal Lord and Savior. Thank You for accepting me and setting me completely free. Help me to live a life that is worthy of You. In Jesus' name. Amen.

Jesus Christ gave this assurance, "Surely I am with you always, to the very end of the age" (Matthew 28:20 NIV). Now that He is with you, know that He will never leave you.

Congratulations for making the most important decision you will ever make! Truly Jesus Christ is with you forever, and He will help you no matter what you are going through. Peace.

Final word

This is about Jesus Christ.

God raised him from the dead, freeing him from the agony of death, because it was impossible for death to keep its hold on him (Acts 2:24 NIV).

This is about you.

I will bring the blind by a way that they knew not; I will lead them in paths that they have not known: I will make darkness light before them, and crooked things straight. These things will I do unto them, and not forsake them (Isaiah 42:16).

This is our future.

The Lord himself shall descend from heaven with a shout, with the voice of the archangel, and with the trump of God: and the dead in Christ shall rise first: then we which are alive and remain shall be caught up together with them in the clouds, to meet the Lord in the air: and so shall we ever be with the Lord. Wherefore comfort one another with these words (1 Thessalonians 4:16-18).

ABOUT THE AUTHOR

Author, Teacher, Evangelist, Pastor, and a conference speaker, Alfred P. Udobong is the President of Global Manifestation Ministries and the senior Pastor of Christ Temple of Manifestation Church in United State of America. Multi-gifted with enormous vision and concern for the body of Christ the church. He has taken the gospels of Christ Jesus to nations of the World in his over 15 years of ministry, and delivering the captives in the name of Christ Jesus, winning souls to the Lord Jesus Christ.

Pastor Alfred and his wife Edna C. Udobong reside in the United States with their son Emem.

He is committed to leading others into their God-given destiny, and making tremendous impact spiritually, economically, socially, in any life that comes across him.

Compassionate in his delivery, he executes a no-nonsense approach to practical Christian living through biblical teachings and personal experience.

Some of his publications include.

How to win souls to Christ,

Last minute to mid-night cry,

Practical deliverance,

Obtaining the Mantle,

Kingdom ambassadors.

RECOMENDATIONS

BE NOT AFRAID is an outstanding book to help every Christian to take a diligent look at their walk with God and put total trust in the Lord rather than to get distracted by the trials and circumstances of life.

Reverend Donald McGaha Senior Pastor
New Life Pentecostal Church
Newnan Georgia U.S.A

Indeed my yokefellow, this book couldn't have come in any better time as this when hearts are bound to fail many people because of the many afflictions as recorded in the infallible word of God in Psalms 34:19.

I am therefore bidding any and every blessed reader of this epoch book to read it until every thing they read turns around to read them right and tell someone else. By this they may have conquered fear and retaining the God kind of faith whose acronym is; Fearless Attitude In Trusting Him (faith). The Lord bless your reading and doing even so amen.

Apostle Victor A Besssong

"Pastor. Alfred presents the truths of the Bible with profound simplicity and theological integrity. This book contains words of hope and encouragement for those who battle with fear. This is a highly readable and a thought provoking book to read."

Dr. Ratna K. Sajja